Advance praise for
A Dating Guide for Catholic Women

I've often wondered where a faithful Catholic single would begin today when considering dating. Now I know. Women should begin with this book. And I suspect that more than a few single men will grow in understanding after a quick study of this book. Sigmund Freud went to his grave wondering, "What do women want?" That's because Amy Bonaccorso wasn't there to say it so clearly.
—Mike Aquilina, author, *Roots of the Faith*

The book that young Catholic women have been waiting for! It offers practical tips for paving the way toward a good Catholic marriage without dodging the tricky issues that come with modern dating life. Amy Bonaccorso weaves in tales from her own dating struggles throughout, which makes the book as fun as it is informative.
—Jennifer Fulwiler, ConversionDiary.com

Honest, refreshing, and extraordinarily objective—I wish I could have read this years ago! This book will inspire you and lead to transformation.
—Magdalena Gutierrez, Archdiocese of Washington, Department for Evangelization

Practical advice on everything from how to meet nice guys to where to go on the first date. A well-paced, energetic book that will have Christian women wondering why nobody has written this before! A very good read.
— Molly N. Cameron, senior editor, Cameron Editorial Services

How to Get to "I Do"

HOW TO
GET TO "I DO"

A Dating Guide for
CATHOLIC WOMEN

AMY BONACCORSO

Foreword by Fr. C. John McCloskey, III

SERVANT
BOOKS

PUBLISHED BY ST. ANTHONY MESSENGER PRESS
CINCINNATI, OHIO

Cover design by Connie Gabbert
Cover image copyright © istockphoto.com | Nina Vaclavova
Book design by Mark Sullivan

LIBRARY OF CONGRESS CATALOGING-IN-PUBLICATION DATA
Bonaccorso, Amy.
How to get to "I do" : a dating guide for Catholic women / Amy Bonaccorso.
p. cm.
Includes bibliographical references and index.
ISBN 978-0-86716-952-2 (pbk. : alk. paper) 1. Man-woman relationships—
Religious aspects—Catholic Church. 2. Dating (Social customs)—Religious
aspects—Catholic Church. 3. Courtship—Religious aspects—Christianity. 4.
Mate selection—Religious aspects—Catholic Church. I. Title.
BX1795.M34B66 2010
241'.6765088282—dc22
2010023860

ISBN 978-0-86716-952-2

*The names of the people in this book have been changed, with the exceptions of
Mother Marija, Attilio Bonaccorso, and Fr. C. John McCloskey, III.*

Published by Servant Books, an imprint of St. Anthony Messenger Press.
28 W. Liberty St.
Cincinnati, OH 45202
www.AmericanCatholic.org
www.ServantBooks.org

Printed in the United States of America.

Printed on acid-free paper.

10 11 12 13 14 5 4 3 2 1

. . . contents . . .

. . . acknowledgments . . .

A very special thank-you to my husband, Attilio Bonaccorso, Jr., for supporting me with my writing, being the first reviewer, and contributing his own creativity to the book. Thanks to acquisitions editor Cindy Cavnar for giving me this opportunity and walking me through the publishing process. Thanks to God, my family, Molly N. and Jim Cameron, Lance Cummins, Fr. C. John McCloskey, Eliot Brenner, Fr. Bill Gurnee, Mother Marija, Richard Basch, Brian Barcaro of Catholicmatch.com, Mike Aquilina, my muses, and everyone else who has encouraged me!

foreword

What's a serious Catholic woman to do…to get to "I do"? Never has it been so difficult to find a man to marry, much less one with whom to share one's faith. The average age of marriage is considerably higher than ever before in the United States. The median age at first marriage is about 26.5 for women and 28 for men, up from about 20 and 22 in 1970. The culture of rampant promiscuity, largely fueled by the availability of contraceptives, has left the "Not till marriage" norm in tatters. As many as 70 percent of engaged Catholic couples are living together when they sign up for their Pre-Cana classes. In earlier and earthier times, that was referred to as "shacking up."

The high level of divorce among Catholics means that women have grown up witnessing many marital breakups, perhaps even those of their own parents and near relatives. As I can testify from pastoral experience, many thousands of Catholic women who are attractive, pious, intelligent, and well educated, and who range in age from their late twenties up to forty and beyond, simply cannot seem to find a Catholic spouse. And all the while they hear the inexorable biological ticking clock, mercilessly shortening their time to bear and raise children.

What's a woman to do? Well, as a priest I would say the expected and obvious. Be a woman of prayer who frequents the sacraments and meditates on Scripture. Follow the teachings of Christ and his Church regarding chastity and modesty to attract the type of man whom you presumably want to meet, fall in love with, marry, and live happily ever after with, hopefully blessed with children, until death do you part. (Yes, it still happens and can happen for you.) And remember that the sacrament of holy matrimony not only "ties the knot" but also carries with it the supernatural sanctifying graces toward growth in holiness that Christ intended when he blessed the young couple of Cana with his presence at the beginning of his public ministry.

Many books have been published in the United States on Catholic marriage. This is not at all surprising, given the centrality of this sacrament for the growth of the Church. After all, there are converts by the tens of thousands in our country every year, but the great majority of Catholics come into the world through the marital embrace. At the very moment of conception, ensoulment takes place. From that point the child only awaits birth and baptism to become enrolled among the saints who are fortified through life by their membership in the Church and participation in its sacramental "cradle-to-grave" spiritual health care. However, marriage is not simply a way to populate heaven; it is also divinely ordained as a means for the spouses to grow in mutual holiness. This is a commitment that lasts until "death do us part."

St. Thomas Aquinas, the Angelic Doctor, tells us that achieving happiness is our natural purpose in life: everlasting happiness in heaven and relative happiness in this life. For 98.5 percent of the Church, that relative happiness and at times even bliss is found in a sacramental marriage that is unitive, open to life, and indissoluble. Marriage is not simply what men and women do to make babies and care for them. It is something much higher, a vocation, a specific call from God to holiness. Along with the spouses' lifelong commitment comes the Church's natural and supernatural help to reach that goal.

Pope John Paul II had a vast pastoral experience with young people and young couples as a parish priest and college professor, before his selection as bishop and then pope. Indeed, throughout his life he kept in touch with many couples whom he had counseled and whose marriage vows he had witnessed. Out of these experiences, he developed his magnificent theology of the body. This almost certainly will be recognized in the future as a true development of doctrine, not only concerning the sacrament of marriage but also concerning the vocation to celibacy. For John Paul II understood both marriage and celibacy as gifts of God and to God.

Having said all that, Amy Bonaccorso, a convert to Catholicism who was deeply influenced by the papacy of John Paul II, brings us to the reason why you picked up this book: to receive concrete advice on how to find a spouse. She does a magnificent and exhaustive job of drawing not only from her vast experience in "the dating game" but also from her many conversations with friends and occasionally even her husband. From the first date down to preparations for the marriage ceremony and reception, it is all here, written with deep insight, many personal anecdotes, and good humor.

Amy did find "her one parking space." (You will understand this expression when you read the book.) In addition to her intended audience, my guess is that more than a few men will be reading this book with great profit. After all, one of men's perennial questions is "What do women want?" Amy Bonaccorso provides one very good answer.

—*Fr. C. John McCloskey III*

chapter one

LIVING IN THE REAL WORLD

Being a Christian woman in the dating world poses unique challenges. I know because I was a Christian dater for nearly ten years.

I wasn't the girl who aspired to be like the movie star with kids outside of marriage. I wanted a strong Catholic husband who would guarantee a wholesome life in the suburbs. Ultra-liberal living arrangements and one-night stands were anathema to me.

It wasn't that I didn't see different possibilities; I could have gone in many directions. I was raised in a spiritual but irreligious household and had diverse friends growing up. In college I had two conversions. For a while I hung out in nondenominational student groups and eventually considered myself Baptist. Then I became a Catholic. Although sometimes confusing, this winding road I followed meant I was well rounded by the time I was twenty-five. I tried to synthesize the best of everything I learned as I sought a husband.

In my efforts to choose the right husband, I sought advice from priests, ministers, and other people who were passionate about the virtues of holding out for the "right one." I came to believe that the right one should be:

- ✓ Catholic, like me
- ✓ Devout
- ✓ Chaste
- ✓ Building a good career
- ✓ College educated
- ✓ Marriage minded
- ✓ Physically attractive

Additionally I wanted him to be willing to support a traditional family structure, in which the mother is able to spend time at home with young children.

Sound familiar?

None of the things mentioned on "the list" are bad things. They are all desirable traits. However, it is easy to assume that good character, kindness, and strong ethics automatically come as part of a package deal when someone is religious. Of course Catholic women want a man who is both religious and of good character. Ideally there is overlap. But life is known to throw us curveballs.

I got a reality check through what I regard as a near-death experience.

FOOL'S GOLD

I thought I had triumphed when I met a man who seemed to match the aforementioned checklist. Let's call him John.

At around the time that we began to talk more about our relationship and future plans, I became very ill. At first it didn't seem like anything serious, so I kept going out on dates with John. But one thing after another went wrong, until finally a coworker said, "Amy, you're falling apart. Leave early and go to a doctor." The doctor initially failed to correctly diagnosis me, which meant that my illness grew much worse for some time.

John was in contact with me off and on. While he was initially sympathetic, my situation meant that I could not cuddle, kiss, or even maintain normal conversations. He soon grew impatient.

After a few days I realized that I was not getting any better and arranged another doctor's visit. I decided that if this doctor could not help me, I would have to go to the emergency room. As I discussed my options and symptoms with John over the phone, his voice grew callous, and he seemed to shrug his shoulders. "Sounds like you have a lawsuit," he said. He was tired of my being sick, tired of hearing about my discomfort, and no longer wanted to be involved.

Alone and afraid, I struggled to focus as I drove to the doctor's office that day. I hardly had energy to ponder the communication breakdown that had just occurred with John. Thankfully, a test revealed that I had a raging bacterial infection. I got the right antibiotics and slowly recovered. It turned out that the illness could have become deadly if I hadn't repeatedly sought treatment.

I recovered, but John's affections never recovered. The guy who had been head over heels for me weeks before became a wall of ice. I felt as if I was the last person on his priority list and had to call my parents, who lived some distance away, to come help me on several occasions.

I did everything I was supposed to do in terms of selecting the right kind of Christian man. I read the right books, attended the right events, used the right litmus tests, was on the right online dating sites, said the right prayers, but this is where it got me: neglected during my time of need.

My situation was not unrivaled. A male colleague of mine told me that this same scenario happened to him when he was dating. While he was seeing a devout girl, he became severely ill and was hospitalized. Although she was nearby, she found every excuse not to visit or help him when he was suffering. As we shared our grisly details, we were both surprised at how similar our experiences were. Someone who overheard our exchange commented that when we think we've been through something unusual, it often turns out to be an experience that many people have gone through before us.

My colleague and I agreed that during our illnesses it didn't matter that the people we were dating were religious, since we didn't experience their faith through their actions. Their words were empty to us when it mattered most. Their church involvement scandalized us because it appeared they were just going through the motions. Trust me. When you're on your deathbed, anything superficial instantly loses its appeal. You'll thoroughly appreciate traits like generosity, compassion, and loyalty, while the excuses people make to save face for poor behavior will just make you feel worse.

During my trauma my father reminded me of the "in sickness and in health" vow that people say when they get married. Tough situations help you decide if someone is spousal material, so maybe this incident was really a blessing in disguise. A doctor even added his two cents. He said, "You're obviously in severe pain and in bad shape. If this guy can't see that, it's better you found out now."

Although at first John seemed like solid gold, for me, he was really fool's gold.

WHEN THE CHECKLISTS DON'T WORK

After this trauma and other disappointments, I started to ask more questions and connect some dots. I evaluated my experiences from numerous vantage points to try to understand the Christian dating problem. Many good Christian women who followed the prescribed Christian dating formulas were getting similar results. It just wasn't working. They ended up with jerks or didn't find anyone at all. Of course, not everyone goes through these trials and tribulations, but I think more women go through the crucible than necessary.

I know dating is difficult overall, but I found something unusual about the Christian dating scene: hypocrisy and rigidity, the results of people desperately trying to fit the definition of "good Christian" on the surface. This obsession with projecting the right image can supersede deep prayer, understanding, and humility. What we end up with is a pool of people who seem to be spiritual and filled with integrity but who try to fulfill the letter of the law without embracing the spirit of the law.

Both hypocrisy and rigidity deny the humanity of others in a dating relationship. When people feel that their true selves are not good enough, they become hypocrites, hiding behind a mask of righteousness. It's hard to connect with someone who lives behind a mask! People should put their best foot forward, but I am talking about *Phantom of the Opera*-style masks that really hide too much. As Mother Marija of the Holy Annunciation Monastery in Sugarloaf, Pennsylvania, once told me, "We cannot be faithful to a self we do not know or are trying to cover up. For the phony there will only be disaster."

Rigidity doesn't allow people to grow in their relationships naturally—it locks them in formulas and formality. This brings tension and negativity, which can actually destroy a relationship that was promising in the beginning—and keep you single forever.

My Achilles' heel was rigidity. The litmus test I used on my dates was that of doctrinal integrity. They had to be in compliance! Somehow I thought that would guarantee me a good spouse. I learned that while I wanted a good Christian man, I needed honesty and transparency just as much. It's better for someone to say, "Well, I don't know that I really agree with that!" than to lie and say, "Oh, yes, we're on the same page." And while I wanted my life to be in accord with Catholic teaching, it turned out that being compassionate and understanding is also essential. In other words, I needed to live in the spirit of the law rather than the letter of the law (where compassion is an afterthought).

THE FLAVOR-OF-THE-WEEK BOOKS I READ, THE ADVICE I GOT

I was attracted to the "how to date" books, but I found that the standard formulas given to Christian women for finding a husband don't work for everyone. In fact, I think some of the stamped and sealed advice keeps them single longer. I do not doubt that the authors have the very best of intentions. Nevertheless, some of the advice isn't reality-based and lacks credibility.

• *No dating.* While some popular books about Christian courtship are not as extreme as others, some people are striving to strike the word "dating" from our vocabulary. Dating is viewed as a practice that encourages promiscuity and secluded trysts. I didn't find this always to be true. Many dates are innocent trips to restaurants or volunteer activities, and they consist of wholesome conversation. Some one-on-one time is necessary; how else can two people determine if they can live with each other for fifty years?

• *Let Dad manage your life for you.* Sometimes included in the courtship philosophy is a recommendation that women rely on their fathers, regardless of their age, to weed out bad apples and weigh in on which men should be permitted to court them. A thirty-five-year-old professional woman has every right to ask her father's opinion about a man, but she has no business asking him to manage her relationships for her. After all, you don't want to set a bad precedent for parental meddling in your marriage. Let Dad live his own life and you live yours. You will be the one who says the marriage vows, not your father.

• *Beware of lifelong singles.* Some Christian dating advice comes from people who are lifelong singles. If they feel called to marriage and aren't married, it would seem that they aren't qualified to give much dating advice, right? Don't listen to people who don't know what they're talking about.

The best advice I got was from women who were already in committed relationships and had weathered the common storms. They were good listeners and supported their female friends. These women were intimately familiar with the typical relationship obstacles, the solutions, the patterns, and the resulting marriage problems when issues were not resolved early on.

I also got good advice from my spiritual directors. One urged me to be less critical of the men I dated, and another, Fr. C. John McCloskey, basically told me to hurry up when I was lagging behind in indecision. He asked, "How old are you?" "Ummm... twenty-five," I replied. His eyes lit up. He said, "OK, you still

have time, but you need to get moving, get online, get out there."
Of course, this doesn't mean that older women can't have wonderful marriages. He just knew that I very much wanted children of my own.

Fr. McCloskey is a former stockbroker, so I think he had a firm understanding of the demands of secular life. He took some of the mystery out of relationships for me. He said, "Finding a man is just like finding a parking spot in New York City. It can be hard and take a while, but you can do it."

LESSONS LEARNED

This book is designed to pass on my most important lessons learned. I got tired of watching women go through the test that dating has become and then ride away into the sunset once they found their husband, leaving the rest of us to figure it out for ourselves. Thanks, gal pals!

In addition to learning how to navigate relationships with the many types of men I met and dated, I learned several lessons that can save you time and frustration. Here are some quick tips for you to consider as you read the book.

1. *Discern your vocation and life purpose for real.* You need to decide, with some level of certitude, what your calling is. Don't waste time by bouncing off and on vocation paths for years. Do your homework and make a decision. If God calls you to marriage, take the vocation seriously, and pursue it with passion. This inner knowing will empower you more than any self-help book.

2. *Stay rooted in reality.* It's usually hard to find a man who meets all of your expectations right off the bat. Acknowledging that reality will help you date in a more realistic and rational

manner. Resist the temptation to idealize a future spouse and compare every man you meet to your idealization. Marriage is an earthly pursuit; it can't exist only in your imagination.

3. *Your biological clock counts.* Ignore anyone who advises you to disregard your biological clock. If you are called to marriage and having children (and a Catholic marriage must be open to having children), you have a time limit when it comes to pregnancy. Don't rush and marry someone who isn't right for you, but do recognize that nature has given you some dating advice already.

4. *Share the lessons you learn.* If you learn something valuable about finding a good husband, pass it on to other women. Your openness will encourage them to share what they have learned with you. Get together for a meal and share experiences. Write an article, start a blog, or offer your insights in other ways.

That's what I decided to do, and you are holding the results in your hands. And to help provide a male perspective throughout the book, I have added sidebars for comments from my husband, Attilio.

chapter two

DISCERNMENT IS EMPOWERMENT

Catholics spend much time praying for religious vocations. What about discerning a call to marriage? A profession? These are just as important, and they deserve the dignity of discernment as well.

I have seen too many people fracture committed relationships because of confusion over their vocation, so I like to talk to daters about discernment. For your own sake and the sake of those around you, you need to discern your vocation responsibly—and put a time limit on it. Before you embark on trying to catch a husband, make sure marriage is truly what you want.

A vocation is meant to facilitate your relationship with God and your path to holiness. If you choose marriage, you'll grow in holiness through your relationship with your husband and children.

In addition, you should decide on a profession based on what your true talents are. Being professionally capable will give you the independence to make the best decisions about marriage.

My First Lessons on "Callings"

The first time I heard about discernment was at a Christian student union in college. People said, "I feel called to do this," if they were inspired through prayer to pursue a degree program, ministry, or other goal. An initial calling should be tested though.

If the calling didn't make sense, people would question its authenticity. This was their informal role as part of the Christian student community. For instance, there was a young man who appeared to be mildly disabled. He wanted to be a doctor. He faced significant obstacles on this path because his disability could make it hard to complete medical school and lead to problems when dispensing medications. A mix-up or wrong dosage could seriously hurt someone.

He was known to mix things up. One time he forgot to set the parking brake on his car, and it ran into a tree. Everyone was thankful for the tree because without it, the car would have rolled into a busy two-lane road. In light of that accident and other occurrences, some people gently nudged him to rethink his decision to be a doctor. A career in medicine just didn't appear to be a good fit for him.

Another man felt called to be a minister. He was passionate about his faith, but he didn't have the maturity that one would expect of a minister. As a consequence people urged him to reconsider his "call" many times. This angered him. Well, if the people you seek to serve through your supposed call question the wisdom of your path, hear them out. A true vocation should be like getting the right pair of shoes.

Usually the people around you will support a true calling or vocation. A friend of mine said that a calling is like a plant that is established in the right climate and soil. A cactus, for instance, thrives in the desert, rather than a moist and shady environment. Friends and family will usually recognize a good fit.

FORMALIZED DISCERNMENT TO RELIGIOUS LIFE

Later I learned how single Catholics discerned a call to celibate religious life—through discernment retreats and other formal activities.

I was attracted to convent life and the spirituality of the mystics. St. Thérèse of Lisieux, my patron saint, was a creative young woman when she entered a Carmelite convent. Likewise, I thought religious life was a cool thing to consider.

As I toyed with this idea, I researched convents and joined the Secular Carmelites, a lay branch of the order, whose members live out Carmelite spirituality in the secular world. I took part in the monthly meetings and prayed the prescribed daily prayers. Most of the women in the group (there were very few men) were older, married, and had children.

Many of the Secular Carmelites regretted not discerning religious life when they were younger. Some of them would say, "If only…". Their regrets made me do a good job at discerning, because I didn't want to share them.

Finally, in 2002, I visited a Carmelite convent in order to make a real decision. I had dabbled with theology school, had just accepted a full-time government job, and was experiencing some anxiety over not knowing what I was supposed to do with my life. I chose an Eastern Rite convent in Sugarloaf, Pennsylvania, which was founded by Fr. Walter Ciszek (author of *With God in Russia* and *He Leadeth Me)* and Mother Marija, the mother superior.

Mother is a phenomenal woman, but I hated the vegetarian diet and kneading bread. I really missed my makeup, my music, and surfing the Internet. I was more "of the world" than I had thought, and we decided that the cloister probably wasn't for me.

You can rely on God to provide synchronicities that light the way. For example, I received a sense of direction through a book about St. Thérèse. The book included photos of locks of hair that belonged to Thérèse and her mother, Zélie. I adored Thérèse's light brown, curly locks. I noticed, though, that my hair resembled her mother's straight, deep brown hair. This inspired me to recognize that in some ways I was more like Thérèse's mother. Zélie had aspired to be a sister in a religious order but ultimately accepted a vocation to marriage and children. This insight helped me accept that I wasn't meant to stay at the convent either.

Closing one door and opening another can have a foreboding feel. Since I still had a little bit of indecision, Mother said, "We'll let the bird fly out of the cage, and if the cage is really home, the bird will fly back." She meant that I would flutter back to the convent if it was really for me. In the meantime she advised me to date, to quit the Secular Carmelites, and basically to act my age. When there is indecision, sometimes you need to test your most natural instincts. God's will and gravitational pull have a way of working in tandem when it comes to vocations.

A Call to Marriage

I remember when I finally took my call to marriage seriously. I had been dating for a few years and was sitting in a restaurant with a girlfriend. She was telling me how she was content to never get married if she couldn't find someone who measured up to her expectations. "I won't settle for less," she said. "It's not worth it to me."

She, like me, was devout. I noticed, however, that her rigidity made it difficult for her to understand the complexities and imperfections of real relationships. She was impatient with people's human weaknesses. On the positive side, she could be serene and prayerful at her best, almost angelic in her purity.

While I would normally have seconded her reticence to settle for a mortal man, I suddenly said, "No! I know God wants me to marry and have kids. I can feel this in my bones. I know that I have to do what he's calling me to do. How could I ignore a call to a vocation? Wouldn't that be wrong? Holding out for perfection won't work, because nobody is perfect."

She looked surprised, but as I explained my commitment to following God's call, her facial expression softened into sympathy. How could she blame me for wanting to fulfill my life purpose? A flower bulb is meant to blossom in the spring, and likewise each of us has her own purpose in life.

While it may seem as if I was hit with a lightning bolt or instantly enlightened, this is far from true. I had debated these issues internally and pondered my vocation many times. I also struggled with perfectionism. A spiritual director once urged me to remember that no man is perfect and that living with an imperfect man can be a road to holiness in itself.

Many of my girlfriends were wasting too much time on the fence of indecision. I knew I couldn't join them. Many were passively choosing, sometimes unwittingly, to join a secular sisterhood (which I discuss further in chapter twelve). I found their unwillingness to take the middle road, and their commitment to a path of rigidity, incompatible with married life. I knew I had to change my faultfinding ways if I wanted to marry.

WHAT IF I'VE PASSED MY CHILDBEARING YEARS?
A call to marriage is usually driven by a desire for children, but don't rule marriage out if you've passed your childbearing years. Life doesn't stop after a certain age. The companionship of mar-

riage can be a blessing to older women just as much as it is to younger women.

A friend, Meredith, told me about a woman whose husband developed medical problems and passed away unexpectedly. She grieved for a year and began to go to church more often. She was in her sixties, and she met a man at church who was in his seventies. They began seeing each other, and she is now thinking that she would accept a marriage proposal if he proposed. They enjoy each other's company and are like high school kids in each other's presence.

I talk to younger women about their biological clock, but older women should know that their time is valuable as well. Meredith encouraged this woman to remember that none of us know how long we have ahead of us. It's best not to take the time we have for granted and to move in the direction that brings us the most happiness.

Is There a Call to Single Life?

Catholics sometimes debate whether or not the single life is a vocation. Pope John Paul II's apostolic letter, On the Vocation of Women, focuses on marriage and religious life, as well as on consecrated virgins. However, we all know women who never marry or consecrate themselves and still contribute to the world in positive ways.

My Great-Aunt Kathryn was an example. When her fiancé died in a job-related accident, she put aside thoughts of marriage and instead cared for the children in our extended family for two generations. She didn't complain about never marrying, and she valued her role as a caregiver. We call her "the saint of the family" because of her selfless giving. I believe it could be said that she had a vocation to the single life.

If you think you could be called to the single life just because you cannot find a man, think again. That's not the same as a call, especially if you don't like your circumstances. Self-pity and resentment don't signal a genuine call. A real call should fill you with a sense of purpose and pride.

Why Solve the Life-Purpose Puzzle?

When I was in college and discerning whether or not I had a vocation to the religious life, I started to date a guy I met at the library. He was good company, but I finally told him that I might enter the convent. He was mad, because he felt that I should have let him know this sooner. I recommend putting a time limit on your discernment to minimize these occurrences and to keep you moving along.

What if you want to float and be receptive and let the chips fall where they may? I've observed that people use time more productively when they have a clear idea of where they're going. Even a general idea is better than remaining aimless for too long.

Your Education and Career Path

Dating and pondering higher callings are important, but don't neglect your education and career. Statistics show that people with more education are more likely to get married.[1] Your earnings will secure your future and provide stability, and a well-chosen job that complements your talents could cease to feel like work.

A history professor once told me that when he was a student, he wanted to be a physicist but didn't do well enough in the classes to justify moving forward. He acknowledged this and changed to the study of history. Sometimes we may wish to do something, and life events will show that it really isn't for us. I now work with physicists and engineers, and they make their jobs look easy! That's usually the case when you're in the right career field.

Most people have a natural strength. A senior executive told me that he could train a communications person to do a good job of writing press releases on a technical subject. Training a technical person to be a communicator was more difficult. He felt that some people are meant for communications and others aren't. So while it can be beneficial to branch out and try new things, it's also to your benefit to acknowledge your path of least resistance.

ARE YOU A HUNTRESS OR NOT?

Men used to be known as the hunters, but now we have hunt-resses too. Not every woman is a huntress—someone who thrives on professional victories and awards. Try to figure out if you are a huntress or not. It can save you time and money.

I met quite a few young women in Washington, D.C., who pursued expensive law degrees and then didn't want to practice law. What happened? They didn't like the aggressive environ-ment, the corporate culture, or the nature of the work. Don't be pushed into a degree program or career for status or a huge sal-ary. Find something that matches your temperament and skills and that offers some level of job security.

There are many women, of course, who enjoy being attorneys. I met one who loved it, and she is the first woman I heard describe herself as a huntress. Last I heard she was working from home as she prepared to have her first child. Now, that's practicality!

If you want to be a stay-at-home mom, mention this when you're dating. A man needs to know. If he doesn't agree, he probably isn't the guy for you. If he's merely nervous about his ability to financially support your desires, try to find a compromise. You could save money before having children or find a job that allows you to work from home. Be creative and minimize the burden on him by figuring out ways to save money.

Don't let stay-at-home-mom ambitions sidetrack you as a single. Allowing yourself to rot at a dead-end job because you're waiting for a man to come and marry you will make you bitter, and your plan may not pan out. If you marry and choose to put your career on hold, that's fine, but knowing how to support yourself as a single will make you less dependent on others.

When I was looking at career choices, I felt certain that I would want to care for my children full-time at home when the day came. I also thought it likely that I would marry a military man who moved around a lot. I wanted to be sure, however, that I had opportunities to earn money if necessary. Those concerns went into my choice to pursue a master's degree in library science. There are libraries all over the world, they usually pay well, and many have flexible part-time gigs in the evenings and on weekends. When my government career took off, I found an agency that offered part-time and work-from-home options. It's possible to develop a career that offers flexible money-making opportunities

In today's economy many men can't earn enough money to be the sole providers for their families. And you need to consider the possibility that your husband could become seriously ill or lose his job. He may need some financial assistance from you, even if it's only to help with college expenses or add to a retirement fund.

Even if you find that you're able to be a stay-at-home mom for thirty years, your children will benefit from your insights if you know how to choose an appropriate profession. And if circumstances change and you remain single or your marriage ends, you can support yourself.

CAVEATS

What if you decide on a path of action but it just doesn't seem to work out very well? This could indicate that your plan needs to change. When things don't flow smoothly, you have to wonder why. Is it really God's will for you?

Pause and think if:

- everyone hates the guy you want to marry;
- there is a consensus that you're not ready to marry;
- nobody thinks you'll be a good nun, and no convents will take you;
- your friends and family think you're choosing the worst career field for your talents and personality;
- you're not happy at your job, and your managers don't ever give you kudos.

Of course, sometimes you may need to go it alone and ignore the opinions of others. Maybe you're on a different wavelength from your family, for instance. Or maybe you have friends who are toxic and don't have your best interests at heart. If these people say, "No, don't marry him!" take their comments with a grain of salt. You can't always trust your loved ones. Don't put much stock in the opinions of those who are obviously being unreasonable.

chapter three

ONLINE DATING: THE NEW EQUALIZER

A discussion about online dating usually elicits a variety of responses. Someone might say, "Oh, I had a horrible experience online! I don't do that anymore." Others, "Hmmm, I tried it once," or, "Oooh, be careful!" If the person is older, he or she might think that only losers try online dating. The truth is that many people will not admit to creating a profile on a dating site, but it is becoming the most popular way to meet someone special. It's nothing to be ashamed of.

I think most people would prefer to meet someone in person, but since that doesn't always happen on our schedule, putting some eggs in the online dating basket isn't a bad idea. Heck, I met my husband online, but it wasn't the only socializing I did. There were times when I was a true social butterfly, but I got tired of meeting the same people at local social events. I had combed my cosmopolitan city for years, and nothing worked out with any of the men I met.

Online dating is the new equalizer. All are equal in cyberspace: men and women, introverts and extroverts, and people from different geographic locations. Online dating makes it possible to become acquainted with individuals you never could have met otherwise.

WHEN YOU ARE NEW IN TOWN OR TIRED AFTER WORK

My husband struck me as a confident and outgoing Italian guy when I first met him. Hailing from the land of *The Sopranos*, New Jersey, there isn't anything fainthearted about him. Even now he often gets e-mails from old high school friends who want to reconnect with him.

So why was he online? He was new in town. His job and career had taken him out of his normal milieu. Like a lot of people who are new in town, he found the bar scene to be rather unsavory, and cyberspace helped him to make new connections.

It's normal for people in their teens and twenties to leave their hometown to start a degree program, internship, or new job. Seeking out people of a similar mind-set online can make the transition to a new life easier and faster.

"Online dating is the wave of the future," one man I dated said. He added, "People get home from work, and they're tired. Online dating lets them do a more thorough search than any other way of dating. It saves time." Also, when people go out to Theology on Tap or other Christian social events after work, they tend to stick near their friends. Online dating forces you to chat with guys who are available and looking. So in that sense it's really productive.

AN EQUAL PLAYING FIELD FOR EXTROVERTS AND INTROVERTS

Online dating provides a setting that both extroverts and introverts can tolerate. In-person speed dating may terrify an introvert, but an e-mail introduction may be less intimidating, buying a timid person time to warm up to someone. Before you meet a guy from a dating site face-to-face, you'll probably know enough about him to make things less awkward than if you were meeting for a blind date.

The Internet can also offer a certain degree of privacy. Gretchen, a thirty-year-old in the Washington, D.C., area, met her fiancé online. She says, "Your friends don't have to know about it." Sometimes you don't want to make decisions by committee; you want a little bit of breathing room to make your own assessments.

At parties an extrovert will usually dominate and attract the most attention. This is not necessarily the case in cyberspace. All sorts of qualities can be apparent through written material, such as intelligence, cleverness, wit, and spiritual values. On the Internet you don't have to be the type of huge personality that dominates social settings to have others notice your best qualities.

Regardless, you have to have some level of courage to make anything work. When I first started online dating, I was a bit paranoid. I would not reveal my real name until I felt comfortable with the person. When a guy wanted to meet, I would sometimes chicken out. I missed out on meeting at least one guy who seemed decent because of my fears. Things became more fun and interesting once I loosened up a bit and embraced my inner urban diva.

EVEN IN A SMALL TOWN...

I spent most of my dating years on Capitol Hill in Washington, D.C. While it may not seem like a small town, it is. It's not uncommon to pass friends on the street or on the subway in this small but manageable city. You can walk from one side to the other in a matter of hours. A thirty-minute bus ride will also do the trick.

Even in a small town with a thriving nightlife, there is a certain practicality to online dating. Although I lived next door to the Capitol dome, I didn't have a job there. I visited the Senate cafeteria periodically to enjoy some Senate Bean Soup, however, and saw lots of young singles there who held government jobs.

But how was I supposed to meet them if I didn't work in the same buildings? Most of their lunchtime chitchat centered on work and politics. If I didn't happen to meet one of them at a Christian event or other shared social activity, it was hard to connect.

I tended to meet these people randomly in restaurants around the Hill but honestly would have preferred an e-mail introduction first. The Hill guys were rather bold. Some would walk up and talk to me as I was eating at a restaurant or picking up lunch; sometimes they would sit down next to me. One staffer asked, "When guys do this, do you tolerate it?" I did when I was looking for a husband, but it could be rather startling.

One time a staffer flagged me down as I was ordering lunch, and we ate our meal together. I was surprised when he had the nerve to invite me on a pricey vacation with him on the spot. I said, "No, thank you," but as payback for refusing, he left the conversation on a rude and insulting note. This was in a public place!

What I'm trying to convey is that online dating offers you some protections against the wiliness of bold men. There are pitfalls though, too, to online dating.

Don't Misrepresent Yourself!
Without really meaning to, people often misrepresent themselves online. They compose their profiles so as to put their best foot forward, which is well and good, but in the process they end up describing the person they want to be rather than the

person they truly are. They think, "This is the best version of me." That's great, but if they aren't the best version of themselves more than 75 percent of the time, other people are going to get an unexpected surprise. This best-foot-forward-gone-awry scenario happens to the best of us, so be wary as you compose your own profile and as you read the profiles of others.

The trap for a woman is trying to be that ideal woman that every man wants. There is no ideal woman that every man wants. That being said, it's probably the case that many men would prefer to marry a woman who knows how to cook and who is tidy. For example, I knew a guy who broke up with a woman because he couldn't stand her messy apartment. Likewise, my husband says he wanted a wife who could cook. Nevertheless, don't portray yourself on your profile as a fabulous cook and a neat freak if you aren't. Sure, you may want to learn to cook, but if you haven't *yet*, do not mix up present and future.

You should also be transparent about your physical appearance. It's one thing to post a profile photo that is complimentary. It's another to post one that is outdated by ten years or that hides your true appearance in some way. Misrepresenting your appearance can cause major embarrassment.

One man I corresponded with told me that he met a woman who wasn't forthcoming about her weight. She posted only a head shot on the dating site. When he met her, he was unprepared for the fact that she was overweight. The man was of below-average height and had a chiseled appearance from frequent weight lifting. It was not a match. When she begged to know why he didn't want to continue seeing her, he had to tell her the truth, and it wasn't easy. He felt extremely guilty, and she was understandably upset. Why not avoid the whole trauma by being honest in the first place?

Searching for Information About the Person for Context

Conducting an Internet "background check" on a new love interest is not off-limits, nor should it be equated with cyberstalking. Cyberstalking has negative connotations and is generally associated with obsessive love. Most people who use the Internet to learn more about new prospects do it because they want to confirm that people are representing themselves accurately or because they want to learn more about them. In my opinion, when you are meeting people online, searching the Internet for information about them is totally within the realm of normal. Cyberspace is your context and your only frame of reference, so it's fair game.

Even though anything online is public information, people can be sensitive about being searched and might feel that you have violated their privacy by digging too deeply too quickly. So tread lightly when and if you bring up the results of your search with the person. After all, mistakes can happen too. Just because you find a criminal record associated with someone's name doesn't mean it belongs to the person you have met. It could belong to another person who shares the same name, or it could be an error. Retain a healthy sense of skepticism when combing through free databases.

There are valid reasons to do a quick search on someone, but I think it can be awkward to know something about a person if that person has not personally shared it with you. I'm not a good liar, so I always worried that my secret knowledge would show through and I would seem sneaky. Ease your conscience by coming clean if you plan on continuing the relationship with your new date. You could say, "Hey, I searched your name online to learn more about you, and I found this." Maybe you can laugh about it together, and he will understand that you didn't intend to be creepy but that you wanted to make sure you weren't going out with a Ted Bundy.

. . . .

Attilio: Ever seen the movie *Hitch*? Will Smith's character researched women online to help the men. I did the same with Amy.

. . . .

THE BEST PROFILES

Online profiles are a great modern convenience in my opinion. Everyone knows how important a first impression is. With an online profile you have a lot of control over that first impression. Make it accurate and meaningful. Put your heart into it, and have some fun.

Get a good photo. The best profiles have a good photo. I used a professional photographer, but you might want to ask a friend or family member to take pictures of you outdoors or in surroundings that are familiar to you. Look your best but not too different from your everyday appearance if you want to be recognized in person!

A shot of you with friends and family can say a lot about you, but get permission from the other people in a photo before posting it online.

Fill out the template. Websites will have a template for you to fill in with information about yourself and the person you're seeking. Fill everything in! Men who took the time to put together a nice profile will wonder what you're hiding if you don't make an attempt to provide some information about yourself.

. . . .

Attilio: Online dating can be nice because you can read a girl's profile a few times to make sure you know how to approach her.

. . . .

Put some thought into it too. Draft it on paper before typing it into the form and posting it for the world to see. Pray about it, and make sure it's a good reflection of who you are at the present time.

Ask a friend if what you have said about yourself is accurate. Since I'm a multifaceted person, my online profile reflected that. One side of me is quiet and shy; the other side is vivacious and fun-loving. After I wrote that, I thought to myself, "I think this is who I am, but is it really possible to be such a combination of opposite traits?" I called a friend and read the description. He said, "Yep, that's you. You change depending on your mood and the circumstances." Friends can help you stay authentic.

. . . chapter four . . .

REAL LIFE MEETS CYBERSPACE

To find the man you're looking for, be careful not to overload an online form with requirements. If you don't find someone quickly, you'll be deleting the excess requirements anyway (and people will notice), so why not start out with a reasonable number of them? Avoid statements such as "men who (fill in the blank) need not apply."

Some women think that if they send out a vibe for a very specific type of man, God will have no choice but to deliver him. So they invent this idealized man and list all of his imaginary traits, hoping to get the man of their dreams. If he doesn't arrive, they have no backup plan.

Of course, you have to express some preferences, but being too specific isn't always to your benefit, especially when it comes to superficial requirements. Don't say that you will only consider men who have a certain appearance. When I was dating I tended to be most attracted to men with blue eyes, and at one point I quietly assumed I would marry a man with blue eyes. I married a man with brown eyes because he had the best character and was compatible with me. Surprise!

And that's the point. Let God surprise you. Don't be so uptight that you can't recognize the goodness he sends. If he sends a man with brown eyes, don't have a knee-jerk reaction and say, "I'm sending him back because I asked for a man with blue eyes."

Be wary of a man who insists that he only wants to meet someone with blonde hair and blue eyes, even if you have blonde hair and blue eyes. Although I admittedly had a preference for blue eyes at one time, I never said I was *only* interested in people with blue eyes or turned down dates just because a man didn't have blue eyes. Nevertheless, I saw online profiles where men said they only wanted to meet women of a particular hair or eye color. Having preferences is understandable, but requiring certain physical attributes across the board indicates that good character and compatibility aren't being recognized as the cornerstones of good relationships.

I recommend saying that you want a man to have wholesome traits that would make him a good husband and father. Great places to start are good character, a decent job, and someone who wants children. You want someone you can trust, rely on, and have fun with. Be honest if your faith is very important to you and you wish to share it with your spouse. In any culture without a strong tradition of arranged marriage, it's assumed that you want to be somewhat attracted to your significant other, so you really don't have to mention that. It's a given.

. . . .

Attilio: Most of the time the guy is looking for someone who can become his best friend, a woman he can rely on. She should also trust his judgment...at least sometimes.

. . . .

The Websites

I tried a variety of websites when I was dating and want to share my thoughts on them. This is not a comprehensive list: There are many sites available, and new ones pop up all the time.

• *eHarmony:* On eHarmony I typically ended up being matched to men I had already come into contact with on the Catholic dating sites, or they lived so far away that it wasn't practical to pursue the relationship.

Also, eHarmony requires that you jump through a number of canned question-and-answer exchanges before you can have open communication with the other person. This can generate excitement—or extreme boredom if you aren't in the mood to play the game. It may be nice for a beginner who is unsure of herself and doesn't know where to start, but I experienced it as an unnecessary formality I had to get through before I could communicate normally.

• *Catholicmatch.com* and *AveMariaSingles.com:* Catholicmatch.com seems to have more active members than AveMariaSingles.com and is cheaper to join. They also have more social networking options. Catholicmatch.com has a sister site, 4marks.com, and together they have a very modern Facebook-like appeal that I enjoyed. There are articles galore, and it's very easy to make connections on it. The websites make it possible to date and make friends at the same time.

Both Catholicmatch.com and AveMariaSingles.com ask a number of doctrinal questions; the sites are meant primarily for observant Catholics.

• *CatholicSingles.com:* Rather than include specific doctrinal questions, this website has one general statement that users address. It says, "As a Catholic, I consider myself…". The possible answers are "conservative," "moderate," "progressive," or you can identify yourself as a catechumen or non-Catholic. The website offers good information about the requirements for marriage in the Catholic Church but also provides an inclusive atmosphere for Catholics of many persuasions.

• *Match.com:* This one is a free-for-all. People from every religion and background are on this site. While you may not find the most conservative Christian men, you will find plenty of average men with good jobs who have integrity. So keep that in mind before dismissing it.

Be aware that on secular sites, more so than on Christian sites, you'll find the bottom of the barrel. Meticulously read everything on a guy's profile before writing him back. I was stunned when I realized that some of the guys would list "adult" in the movies section, so I began checking each profile for this and for other indicators that they were overly focused on sex. It's an easy way to weed out guys. Obviously, it will be impossible to create a healthy relationship with someone who broadcasts that he objectifies women. That's a blazing red flag.

As you use these or any other dating sites, keep in mind that it's no joke that the Internet, especially online dating, can be addictive. I had friends who did online dating in stints simply to manage its addictive quality. Signing up for three months, going at it full speed, and then taking a break may work for you. If you are more of a long-distance runner, you may stay with online dating sites long-term and just limit the time you spend on the computer every week.

While Internet dating can be productive and fun, don't let it keep you indoors and away from live activities. It's only one basket to put eggs in.

WHEN TO TALK OVER THE PHONE

It usually took me one or two weeks to discover whether or not I had a connection with a guy. I would try to find things we had in common. Did we like the same music? The same saints? The same food? Did he have a degree, a career path? In other words, were we of the same feather? (You know the saying, "Birds of a feather flock together.")

After about one to two weeks, you'll usually talk over the phone or plan to meet in person. Sometimes a phone call would be enough for me to determine if I was really interested. For example, I corresponded with a former seminarian, but when I spoke to him on the phone, my impressions from the first week or so of e-mails fell apart. He came across as irresponsible and naïve. His head was in the clouds. We stopped talking after that, because it clearly wasn't a harmonious match.

LOCALS AND OUT-OF-TOWNERS

Locals may skip the phone assessment, but if you aren't sure about a local person, a phone call can help you decide if you want to meet. By phone you can confirm that the guy you've been writing to matches his self-description, or you can quickly coordinate a date to demonstrate that you're a real person wanting to interact off-line.

Before meeting anyone, be sure that you feel a strong enough connection to endure a two-hour date. If you don't feel that you can be a good conversationalist for at least an hour or so, question whether you need to get to know the person a little better or find someone else.

If someone is from a neighboring city, I'd recommend getting to know each other over the phone and e-mail for perhaps three to four weeks before pursuing the relationship in person.

If the guy lives more than a car ride away, I'd wait maybe four to six weeks. You don't want to waste time and resources on something that doesn't have promise. Try to get as much information as you can via e-mail and telephone first, so you can be sure the travel is worth the investment. You may still take the trip and be disappointed, but if you've invested only a few weeks, it won't be too much time lost.

You should be able to make a decision about someone after two or three months; otherwise you could be leading him on and wasting valuable time. After a few months you start to feel committed even if you shouldn't be. Your heart will get absorbed in the relationship, and it will be harder to make a clean break if the guy isn't right for you. That means it will be more of a struggle to move on and find the right one.

Lodging for Out-of-Towners

If a man is coming to see you from out of town, you should be a good host and help him find lodging.

If you have some friends who have an extra room, that could work. It would also give your friends an opportunity to get to know him and give you their assessment, if you're ready for that. Is he nice? Intelligent? Creepy? When I was dating I didn't have many friends with spare rooms, so I tried to find a hotel that was nearby and economical.

Even if you have a large living space, don't offer the new guy a place to sleep in your house.

Please do be open to the possibility of expanding your scope to out-of-towners. A man I interviewed for a *Washington Times* article told me that he found a compatible match only after he expanded his geographical scope.[2] He resides in the Washington, D.C., area and dated there for many years. After reaching forty and still not finding anyone, he decided to broaden his scope to include New Jersey. His mother lived in New Jersey, and he visited her frequently. He found his match there. His message was, "Don't limit yourself."

But Clicking Happens

There is always an exception to any guidance. Although typically I wrote to a guy for a week or two before meeting him, I was on the phone with my husband within a day or so of first making contact online. In fact, I met him in person the same night we spoke on the phone.

The reason for this was because we had both dated a lot and felt confident about our ability to size someone up quickly. He felt that I was a good catch and didn't think I'd be online long before another man snagged me. Also, it was just before Easter weekend. He was going to visit his family in New Jersey and didn't want me to forget about him over the long break. He asked if I would be willing to meet, and I agreed. We talked for hours, and it clicked.

Clicking happens, so listen to your gut.

The First Meeting

The first meeting should be in a public place, typically on the woman's home turf. Women are still considered the more vulnerable party in dating and should be more concerned about safety. Although men usually take responsibility for choosing the details of a typical first date, the first meeting of a couple who met through an online site can be decided by the woman.

. . . .

Attilio: Meeting in a public place is a totally reasonable and responsible thing to do. If a guy isn't willing to allow a woman a comfort zone, especially on a first date, it might be a warning sign.

. . . .

I typically chose Union Station to meet new guys. Union Station is the Washington equivalent of New York City's Grand Central Station or similar town centers. It has coffee shops, restaurants, and a bookstore, and it is usually jam-packed with people. With its places to sit, space to stroll around, security guards, and interesting conversation pieces, it's the ideal place to meet someone new.

When I lived in the Virginia suburbs, I would use coffee shops or even churches for first meetings. The only downside to coffee shops is that you may have the misfortune of meeting someone with zero social skills and have nosy customers seated next to you. This happened to me once. I arranged to meet a first-time date from out of town at a coffee shop only to discover too late that he spoke with a very loud and indiscreet voice. As I flushed with embarrassment, I glanced around and noticed that customers were clearly taking an interest in the fiasco. I was horrified. One of the employees was a former coworker. Imagine a personal conversation being heard by your neighborhood!

I ended up excusing myself and calling a friend to rescue me for the rest of the evening. He was a big-brother type I had met at a Christian student union in college. He joined us for dinner and steered the conversation in a very general and casual direction. I also had him cut it off at a certain time and drive me home. Letting the guy know that you aren't interested afterward is a delicate process.

There were other times when meeting at the coffee shop was a fabulous idea. I met one man in D.C. who was an excellent conversationalist, and we had an enjoyable first date over coffee and tea. It's still good though to have the option to take a walk if it's evident that eavesdroppers are around.

CANCELING A DATE; THE THREE-DATE RULE

I once had a date with a rather flighty attorney who was quite a socialite. He was a triple threat in my eyes: good job, smiling Irish eyes, and an observant Catholic. I was sick on the night of our date but didn't cancel. This wasn't a good call. I was loopy from cold medicine and had tissues stuffed in my coat pockets. The relationship ultimately didn't work out, and I regretted that I wasn't able to make a better impression that evening. The first few dates are the most important, and you don't want a man to write you off because he saw you when you weren't at your best.

So cancel if you aren't well, if you have severe PMS (let's be honest, we all have those days!), or if you're on medications like antibiotics or antihistamines that make you feel weird or super-sensitive to alcohol.

. . . .

Attilio: Early on in a relationship, a sick date is no fun and should be avoided, but later it should be no problem to stay in and make chicken soup!

. . . .

A lot of daters follow a three-date rule to manage the amount of time they spend on one person and to pace the decision making.

This is true, too, in the online dating universe.

Even with the online interaction and a potential phone call assessment, there is no substitute for in-person communication and interaction. The first date is for information gathering and discovery. If you connect well enough on the first date, a second date is in order, and you will use a finer-toothed comb. Do you really like this guy enough to stay with him long-term? Most people can make an initial decision at the two-date mark. The tougher cases need a third and maybe a fourth date. But any more than that without a tentative decision puts you into tricky territory. It's the territory of "Are you leading me on? What's the deal?"

ARCHETYPES TO AVOID

Here are three quick archetypes for women to avoid. They are valid for both Christian and non-Christian dating sites.

The antisocial socialite. I met this type online a few times— a man who was really into writing long letters to lady friends but who never displayed an interest in anything more. If you become friends with a man who writes you for more than two or three months without mentioning a phone call or in-person visit, ditch him. He's wasting your time. (I don't believe in the validity of online marriages!) Such a relationship won't lead anywhere, and the constant writing without real contact creates a false sense of intimacy.

The real socialite. Some guys are just out there to play the field and don't care how the ladies feel about that. If someone tells you this up-front, be sure to communicate your expectations. Otherwise he could end up dating and kissing lots of girls at one time. If you hit the point where you think the relationship should be exclusive, tell him. If he won't agree, you have to decide to either set him loose or remain one of many love interests and keep it low-key and casual.

The sugar daddy. This is a classic type, and yes, he exists! The guy who showers you with expensive gifts and trips almost immediately expects "something" in return. Even if he's Christian and says he's into chastity, watch out.

WHEN YOU JUST AREN'T THAT INTO HIM

Letting a guy know that you don't reciprocate his interest is hard. It's especially difficult because men have delicate egos and usually make the first move in dating. Before you let a guy down, take a second to think about how hard it must be to stand in his shoes.

With online dating, letting a guy know can be as easy as not responding to an e-mail. This may be appropriate if you haven't been in contact very long. Sometimes guys take the hint and just go on their merry way. Other times they'll e-mail you back and ask why you haven't written them. Then you will have to be honest.

You can say that you just don't feel that he is the right match for you, or that you aren't interested in pursuing the relationship at this time, or maybe discuss a specific issue. If he's super-Presbyterian and you're super-Catholic, you could say that you don't think you could manage that.

I wouldn't tell him that you aren't attracted to him or that you don't like his smell. You want to let him know that you're moving on without killing his self-esteem.

Be ready for him to come back with a stinger, no matter how gentle you are. It happens. Ignore it and move on.

This is not the time to remain friends. Staying friends could mean that you both stay involved in each other's activities, and it can lead to jealousy games. It's a waste of your time if you really intend to move on. Years later, if you're neighbors, then maybe you can become friends again.

If you really like him but have one sticking point, discuss the issue that gives you heartburn pretty early on, even if you haven't yet met face-to-face and you're still writing online. The first few weeks to a month is a good time to discuss major issues that could be obstacles to commitment later. You don't want to be in a relationship that troubles your conscience, so being open early on is in your best interest.

BUT WE ARE JUST PEN PALS
I know a lot about this....

I had one "pen pal" I liked a lot. Let's call him Sean. The problem was that he lived in California, and I lived in Washington, D.C. We were both interested in Opus Dei, a Catholic institution designed to help people find holiness in daily life.

So why even bother with a long-distance relationship? Well, our spiritual directors knew each other, and so although we were on opposite coasts, it seemed as though something could work out for us. This was not blind affection: We had a real-life connection.

The truth is that regardless of our many delightful e-mails and telephone calls, he wasn't willing to come to D.C. and pursue the relationship. I didn't feel any encouragement from him to arrange a trip to California either.

As I moved on and dated other men, he was a great support to me. When I had an encounter with an abusive man, he e-mailed me advice: "I've heard about guys like this; don't take him back, Amy!" It's probably a good thing to have some male advice-givers in the wings, but I don't recommend putting too much stock in a pen pal as husband material if he isn't willing to meet in person. If he turns into a big-brother figure, OK, but don't secretly hold out for him to change his mind and come sweep you off your feet. You could be waiting years. I don't know about you, but I always find it hard to turn off my hopes once I have built them up.

· ·

Attilio: Pen pals are difficult to judge because they can take the time to deliberately craft their written words. But what are they like in real life? Someone could be a great writer but a social idiot. Keep your expectations real, because you could be let down.

· ·

The Bad Apples

In my experience, if profiles prove to be inaccurate, it's usually because people *accidentally* misrepresented themselves or just went overboard with the aforementioned best-foot-forward mentality. There was no true malice. At the same time there are bad people out there who mislead on purpose. Make sure you use your street smarts online, and don't trust someone too quickly.

Be on guard for the common and easy-to-fall-into false-sense-of-intimacy phenomenon. People tend to reveal things about themselves online that they normally wouldn't say to someone they just met face-to-face. Revealing too much too soon isn't safe. Further, no amount of security from an online dating company will completely protect you from people who don't have your best interests at heart.

If you have young children, wait a while before trusting a new date alone with them. I have heard a few stories about child molesters purposely seeking out single mothers so they can have access to their children for criminal purposes.

Being inquisitive without being prying can help weed out the bad apples when you're not sure about something. For instance, one time I corresponded with a guy who said he lived in Canada. I casually asked him who the Canadian Prime Minister was, and he didn't know! At that point I got suspicious. Later I found him listed on the website as coming from somewhere else.

Another man I corresponded with lived in another state. He was a musician, and he wrote songs for me. He also was super weird, and he proposed to me on the phone without ever meeting me. When I asked him questions, I found out that he had done this to many women. Obviously something was wrong with that picture, and I stopped talking to him.

BLOCKING PEOPLE

Remember that if a man harasses you online or freaks you out, you can block him so that he can no longer contact you.

I met one older man online, and the relationship quickly went to personal e-mail addresses, instant messaging, and an in-person meeting. I learned that he had recently gone bankrupt and owed many people money. He also had some spiritual issues that I wasn't able to help him with. Additionally, when I backed away from the relationship, he e-mailed me off and on for years, trying to get an answer from me.

I don't think he was dangerous or a really bad person. But he wasn't the type of person I needed in my life. I was a young college student, impressionable, and on the up-and-up. I was unable to relate to his particular issues and didn't see him in my future. Regardless, he didn't accept that, so I blocked him.

Use the block option with discretion. You don't want to be too quick about it, because it can cause offense and be a permanent solution to a temporary problem. Only use it as a last resort or when something occurs (or reoccurs) that makes it very clear that the person deserves to be blocked.

From my many experiences I can confirm that online dating is a viable way to meet guys. It comes with caveats, though, just as traditional meeting and dating scenarios do.

. . . chapter five . . .

MEETING MEN THE OLD-FASHIONED WAY

So you know that online dating is the wave of the future but would still prefer to meet your future husband the old-fashioned way? If that's you, here are some things to keep in mind.

THE BASICS: LOCATION, LAZINESS, HEALTH, AND WELLNESS
Meeting a potential spouse through your day-to-day social activities is easier in some places than others. I moved from the suburbs to the city when I realized that it was getting harder to meet people my age. Similarly, I work with a gentleman who told me that he once refused a job offer to teach at a university in a rural area because he was looking for a wife. He needed to live in a highly populated area to increase his chances.

If you're having a hard time finding men and you live in a small town, consider relocating to a city. It sounds drastic, but if you're bored and lonely, it might be the best thing for you. A move could energize your social life and also help you get ahead professionally.

To create ample opportunities to meet guys, you can't be socially lazy. Social laziness becomes more of a risk as people get older, but it can happen to anybody.

You should try to get out a few nights a week if you really want to meet people in person. Initially I started with a minimum of two nights a week and worked up to three or four. Eventually I was out six nights a week. This is easier for some people than others. I know I was not the only single doing this, but that much activity can get a little draining and create the need for a long break. Be careful about overdoing it. Your own sanity and balance are just as important as meeting new people.

If there is a health problem that's keeping you indoors, try to address it. I met a few young and healthy-looking women who were struggling with chronic fatigue–like symptoms that made regular outings difficult. One time a friend bailed out on lunch at the last minute because she just couldn't get her energy up.

I can relate to this problem. I had a bout with fatigue when I was around twenty-three, and I knew it was limiting my ability to get out and meet people. I once traveled an hour to get to a social event in the city and all of a sudden felt as if I was going to pass out.

Soon after that I moved to D.C. to eliminate the hour-long commutes, and I also had some doctors evaluate my condition. They couldn't do anything for me because nothing was severely wrong. Fatigue can be a symptom of a wide variety of physical and psychological conditions, and there isn't always a magic pill to instantly fix the problem.

Did I stop there? No, this was my life, and I had to live it! I began seeing an acupuncturist, taking Chinese herbs to increase my energy levels, and drinking more green tea. It worked like a charm, and it's the reason I can maintain a busy schedule to this day.

For other people the answer might be a regular exercise routine or a high protein diet that keeps energy levels up. High-stress jobs can be draining; in those cases something like yoga could be restorative. Other people, sore from sitting at a desk all day, might benefit from a massage every so often to relieve the tension. There are many options, some of which could even lead you to meet new people. Addressing health and energy issues is worth it when you need to get out there.

Become a Joiner, and Get Comfortable in Groups

During my college days and time living in Washington, D.C., I built an active social life through my involvement with various Christian groups. Sometimes it was almost therapeutic to get together with other people in my age group who had similar hopes, values, and dreams.

While my suggestions are by no means exhaustive, they should help you identify some good opportunities if you want to meet new people in person. I share my experiences to familiarize you with the social environments you're likely to encounter.

The lecture circuit. Libraries, churches, universities, and other places of learning often have lecture series open to the public. I have bookish leanings and enjoyed meeting intelligent and articulate people at these events. At lectures I found opportunities to interact with others on an intellectual level, which can be less nerve-wracking than diving straight into relationship-speak. You can find lecture series advertised in church bulletins, in newspapers, in newsletters, on bulletin boards, and on the Internet.

I felt comfortable attending certain more structured events alone—for example, when I was part of an audience facing a podium. I did this often. However, a less formal event, such as one held in a restaurant or a venue with tables and chairs, felt awkward. I recommend avoiding the discomfort by going with a buddy.

In Washington one of the most popular events for Catholics is Theology on Tap. Young adults gather at a pub or restaurant to hear a talk on a theological topic, followed by discussion. It's a relaxed, fun evening and open enough that some non-Catholics will come along if the topic is appealing. The organizers usually have an e-mail list. Always sign up for e-mails! Not only will you get notices about upcoming Theology on Tap nights, but you'll get news about other social events in the area. At the event itself you may find flyers for other social opportunities.

At a lecture, even though many people are there with the silent intention of meeting a mate, they can be shy and reluctant to branch out and meet new people. While it's always possible that some dashing guy is going to be transfixed by your beauty and walk up to you out of the blue at your first meeting, it's more likely that you'll make new connections if you go regularly to a lecture series or a repeat event, slowly building an increasing circle of contacts. Each time, meet someone new, and get in the habit of making introductions. Pretty soon the circle will get larger, and that's when a guy will probably ask for your phone number.

If you have a gregarious personality, do everyone a favor by making as many introductions as possible at these events. The quiet types will praise Jesus for your social skills. People want to pair up, but getting timid folks out of their shells takes time and effort. To get into the small-talk groove, they need several visits, familiar faces, and maybe some good food and adult beverages.

Book clubs. Book clubs can be a great way to make contacts. Usually held at someone's home or a local Christian bookstore, they're similar to lectures in that they have an intellectual bent and provide something to discuss but are usually more tightly knit. This makes it easier to form lasting connections through them.

If you help coordinate them (or any other regular social activity), you'll have access to the e-mail list of potential attendees and get to know names and faces that way. I helped coordinate a book club for Pope John Paul II's *Love and Responsibility* and met the majority of my close friends (and a few dates) through it.

College communities. College organizations sponsor events and weekly opportunities to get together with like-minded students. If you're attending classes, check the bulletin boards and college website. Many people meet girlfriends and boyfriends through college communities, so if you can find one that resonates with you, it's worth your time to get involved.

I have fond memories of one Christian group whose meetings I attended in community college. The minister gave short lunchtime talks, and his church sponsored meals for the attendees. I met a good friend there, and I know that some other students dated people they met at these lunches.

I attended a Baptist student union at a public university and met a guy there who became my boyfriend. Many of my friends seriously dated people they met through the small prayer groups and other fellowship opportunities at the union. It was impossible to get involved there without forming meaningful relationships. Campus Crusade for Christ is also a popular university group, and similar fellowship clubs pop up all the time. A group like this can become a center of your life.

Once I became Catholic, it was the Catholic campus ministry that caught my attention. I didn't find any romance there, but I did meet the woman who became my matron of honor. Even after college I was invited to the Newman Center at a local university to attend meetings of Communion and Liberation, a movement that fosters the growth of Christian maturity among its members. The meetings included discussion and dinner, but most of the attendees were Spanish-speaking, so I eventually dropped out because of the language barrier. Nevertheless it was a great way to meet people and grow spiritually.

Of course there are nonreligious groups too, some of which are academically focused. Those can provide good opportunities to meet people and build friendships on shared interests.

Church groups. Some churches have young professional or singles groups in addition to more traditional organizations. The advertisements will usually give you an idea of the age group they are targeting, like ages twenty-two to thirty-nine. These are a mixed bag. Some of them attract only the super-geeky, while others are high-energy and diverse.

Some suburban churches had groups that made me feel uncomfortable instantly. (Like, "Hmmm…what did I do wrong to end up here? I must be a real loser.") Any group that makes you feel bad about yourself is probably not going to be your thing long-term. However, you could get some decent e-mail list information from the organizer and find out about more palatable social opportunities from there. Always try to take away something of value from these awkward experiences!

City churches tend to cater to young professionals. Their groups were so impressive that I would persuade people who weren't very religious to come and check them out for the sake of good company. As I mentioned previously, some fellows would interrupt my meals on Capitol Hill to introduce themselves. One of those guys seemed lonely, so I told him about the Catholic singles scene. Fast-forward a year later. I saw him at a local church's annual Octoberfest. He was in line with a group of friends to get some German food.

I thought it was great that the D.C. churches had events good enough to attract people from all walks of life, but that also meant that I couldn't assume that every guy I met at these things was there for the best reasons. Unfortunately, some people would poke fun at these D.C. churches for hosting "meat markets." Still, I think inclusive events have their place and offer good opportunities to meet people.

Most communities have a hub or place where there is just a lot of good stuff going on, and the trick is to figure out where those places are. Sometimes these places remain hubs for years. In D.C. St. Matthew's Cathedral has always been a center of social activity. My mother, who wasn't raised Catholic, went to dances there when she was younger and was surprised when I told her that many years later their events still attracted crowds of singles like a magnet.

If you're registered with a particular parish, you can still be involved in your parish while sampling the social activities at other churches. I think most pastors understand that singles parish-hop for the social activities and that this is a temporary condition for most people. This restlessness is good, because continually hanging out with the same group of people isn't going to help you. When you're trying to find a spouse, you need to cast your net as widely as possible. When people marry they typically settle back into a home parish and put down some roots.

Speed dating. I never went speed dating, but it sounds like a neat idea for someone who wants in-person introductions. At a speed-dating event, you get a few minutes each with several single men to briefly introduce yourself. If you click you can arrange to see each other again.

Work. It used to be considered a faux pas to date people from the same workplace, but today it's not uncommon, and it can be successful. At the same time it's better to date someone who isn't in your office or work unit, so you won't be forced to work with them every day in the event of a breakup.

Charitable causes. Helping others is a great way to get involved with a group of kindhearted people. Mentoring programs, soup kitchens, animal shelters, prison ministries, and many other charitable causes are always looking for volunteers.

I mentored girls in the context of a formal group in my area. A partner organization sponsored boys. There were occasional opportunities for the men and women who mentored the children to meet each other. It was a good way to meet people who gave up their personal time to help others. It was also a good way to nurture my maternal instincts.

Not every charitable activity is appropriate for women, especially young and attractive ones. Be open-minded but not so open-minded that your brain falls out! For instance, writing letters to men who are incarcerated might not be the best choice. When I was hanging out with a Christian student group, the resident minister encouraged students to write letters to a guy who was in jail. I felt sorry for the guy and did it, but he got too candid with me. He probably thought, "Ohhh, I have a nice girl writing me. Maybe I can have a girlfriend when I come out." The guy I was dating at the time didn't appreciate it. It would have been better if men had written the letters of support.

When people are begging for volunteers, they are advocating for those in need, not necessarily keeping an eye out for the risks involved for those who volunteer. If you want to do prison ministry, stick with writing to women, and talk to other people who have experience with it.

Years later I met a guy who was deeply involved with charitable causes and spent a lot of his time helping at a halfway house in a sketchy part of town. He was so committed to the world of selfless giving that he quit his high-paying day job. When I began hanging out with him, he wanted me to join him in his charitable pursuits. I'm sure that he just wanted his girlfriend to be his best friend—a true companion and helpmate. That seemed cool at first, but it evolved into his venturing into heroic territory where I didn't feel comfortable.

The incident that brought things to an end would have put my safety in jeopardy. Some people offered their basement as an overnight homeless shelter, on the condition that a responsible, non-homeless adult stay there overnight as well. This guy volunteered to sleep on the floor with the homeless people in order to secure the basement. Guess who he invited to sleep on the floor with him and the homeless? I said no and stopped seeing him. No matter how much you like someone or want to help out, always put your safety first.

Formal religious groups. If you're the type of woman who wants to marry the kind of guy who is super-holy and also looking to get married, you might think you should begin your hunt within the most austere religious organizations. Please think twice about this. A guy who is serious about getting married may not be spending his time where you think, and you need to think about how you spend your time as well.

Joining is fun, and so is creating a unique spiritual identity for yourself. Some of these formal organizations—such as secular branches of religious orders—are not ideal for singles and won't provide the kinds of social activities you need if you are to meet your spouse.

For example, the most popular secular orders enable lay-people to live out the spirituality of the Carmelites, Franciscans, or Dominicans in the secular world. You'll get their very best sales pitch if you attend one of their meetings, usually held at a church or monastery. Go home and think about it before impulsively signing up.

Before joining a secular order, think about how it will impact your search for a husband. Will your commitment to the organization eclipse your goal of getting married and having a family? Formal groups come with a full load of scheduled prayers and meetings. The meetings may fall on Sundays. What happens if your boyfriend wants you to join him for a summer barbecue after church, and it just happens to be your order's Sunday meeting day? If you choose the meeting, the guy might think you aren't that into him, and if you skip the meeting, the order will think you aren't that into them. Also you may be committed to the Liturgy of Hours. What if your date interferes with those prayers? Are you going to pull out your breviary for evening prayer at a restaurant or explain that you must end the date early?

These are the kinds of conflicts that could happen if you try dating and pursuing a lay branch of a religious order at the same time. It's not always practical and could create a crisis of conscience.

There are other semiformal groups that are less demanding for laypeople. When you're dating, it's best to find something with flexibility, because you'll need it when you get into a serious relationship.

View visits to groups that require serious commitments as taste tests when you're single and looking for a husband. This is not the most opportune time for life-altering promises, unless, of course, it's matrimony. When you're young, give yourself time to discover everything that's out there.

If you are drawn to a particular order, you can always collect artwork and books that remind you of their charism, and you can pray their prayers. You can also go on pilgrimages with a group of people, if that fits your budget. There are plenty of devotions you can embrace and still postpone a serious commitment to a formal group until you are really sure how it will fit into your life.

FAITH-BASED ACTIVITIES ARE DIFFERENT FROM BARS, BUT...
Social events with religious groups are different from the bar scene in many ways. At the same time, I learned that even within the Christian student groups I was part of, there was debauchery behind the scenes. It wasn't openly bragged about, and it was easy enough for me to avoid, but it was still there. I knew girls who attended conservative Christian colleges and told tales of

promiscuity, rape, and manipulation. There is no requirement to take a lifestyle polygraph test before you enter a Christian social group, whether in college or after, so stay alert.

Christian groups that seem overly demanding or cultish present another problem. Singles are susceptible to falling into such groups if they are lonely. In some cases members will descend on newcomers like over-friendly hawks and display superficial smiles in unison. They will urge you to immediately sign up for everything and wonder why you don't come to every event. The recruiters can e-mail and call you repeatedly, like insurance salesmen. If it's too aggressive and you feel too much pressure to conform to a group's individual flavor and routine, back away.

Also, remember that church groups lay out the welcome mat for everyone, and rightly so. You will find yourself conversing with people with severe handicaps, learning disabilities, and other issues, who hope that they will find kind faces and potential friends at church. You might need to learn how to sensitively handle guys with developmental disorders.

If you're a student, for example, and one of these men develops a crush on you and follows you around campus, do you panic and report him for stalking, or do you talk to the campus minister first? If you met the man at a religious event and have the feeling that he's just socially inept, it's probably a better idea to talk to someone first. Perhaps he can receive counseling before he gets in real trouble.

What if a guy with an emotional disorder asks you out? Don't agree to date him out of pity. Kindly say that you're complimented but not interested. A white lie might even be appropriate if it helps get you out of the situation. If you're nervous about how he might react, tell your friends and family, or the campus minister if you're a student. Of course any situation that makes you fear for your safety should be reported to security and local authorities.

Do Something You Love

I have noticed that some Christian women limit themselves to church activities and think that they must meet their husband in a church environment. This hoped-for meeting doesn't always happen! Embracing your hobbies and interests can bear fruit as well, providing a good way to meet someone who shares a passion with you. It can also help you develop your talents and give you something interesting to talk about when you're out. Not every conversation needs to revolve around religion and the church.

Follow your heart and do something you love. Art schools offer a variety of classes. You could volunteer at a theater if you love shows. Continuing education opportunities at colleges and universities can put you back into an atmosphere of learning and intellectual exchange and give you access to elite libraries. If you are into politics, consider joining the local political groups. The singles will campaign together and sometimes keep meeting or going out when campaign season dies down. Studying another language can widen your travel options and perhaps expand the pool of men you can date. I once knew a woman who met her husband on a vacation in Greece; sudden and romantic surprises can happen.

Even taking a class to learn a few more recipes can be just what you need. My mom worked for a man who met his wife at a cooking class. She lucked out because she got a husband who loved to cook for her!

If I hadn't met my husband when I did, I probably would have taken a jewelry design class. Both my mom and I noticed that whenever I went to a craft show, I instantly clicked with the male jewelers. I like the idea of making my own jewelry too, so it's just another option that would have made sense for me.

Sign Up for the E-mail Lists

Remember that even if you really want to meet someone the old-fashioned way, it will be hard to avoid the Internet completely. A lot of announcements and private invitations for social events come out via e-mail and Facebook. This is true even in big cities. I've said it before: Get on every e-mail list you can!

People just don't have the time to sit on the phone and call twenty people anymore. And although mailed invitations are super-classy, they are increasingly rare. Busy people usually don't have up-to-date address information for all of their friends and acquaintances, and as the cost of postage rises, many prefer e-mail for the cost savings.

Still...Put an Egg in the Online-Dating Basket!

What if you have an appointment and need to leave an event early—and the guy who has been studying you from afar can't ask for your number fast enough? He's sitting there thinking, "Drat! She was so cute, she didn't have an engagement ring.... I really wanted to get to know her better."

Well, if you're both on Catholic online dating services and on the e-mail lists, he could do some investigating to contact you that way and introduce himself. People on dating sites will recognize faces from photos on the profile and log on when they get home to connect the dots. You could get an e-mail that says, "Hi, Ashley. Weren't you at the event at St. Pat's last night?

I really loved the talk. Do you think we could get coffee next week?" It happens!

If you want the dates, you need to make yourself available. If you wait too long and miss these opportunities, you'll see him at the next event with another girl, and then you'll be the one saying, "Drat!"

Don't assume that you'll meet someone when you least expect it and that you shouldn't do anything to help matters along. Some women do find that the right man comes along with no effort on their part, but others are still single after thirty years and don't know why. That's why it's so important to put eggs in many baskets.

chapter six

MODERN DATING ETIQUETTE

Times have changed since our parents and grandparents dated. While women are still regarded as the fairer and more vulnerable sex, dating etiquette has evolved slightly to reflect changes in our culture and society.

WHO ASKS FOR THE DATE?

It's still usually the expectation that the man ask a woman for dates. This sets him up for being the one to propose. I stood by this tradition because it showed me a man really wanted to be in the relationship and had the motivation to work for it.

I don't hear many stories of women asking guys for dates. If they try to take the lead too often, women risk latching onto men who won't take responsibility for relationships. But a woman should assure a man of her interest in him. Many guys will say that they appreciate it when a woman gives signals that she wants a date. Smiling, eye contact, and friendly conversation will give him a clue, and some will act quickly on it. I tutored a few women on this when no guys were asking them out.

If you're feeling brave and want to get to know a guy, you could glance at your watch during a conversation and say, "Hey, do you have time for a coffee?" Say it as if you are going anyway, whether he joins you or not. Or, "Do you wanna see this art exhibit with me?" It should be done in a very casual, not-a-big-deal manner. Don't say *date* or get too nervous. He could politely decline. Or he could say, "Yeah, sure. Let's go," and not miss a beat. If he has a good time, it's his turn. He should ask you for a date next time.

While some men may be flattered when a girl takes the wheel, they may not be motivated to pursue her. If you are too aggressive, it can make him feel inadequate or take the fun out of the chase. A lot of people just have a natural respect for tradition too.

WHO PAYS FOR THE DATE?

My dad always told me that if a guy invited me out, he paid. This is a traditional mind-set, and it still works for some couples. It usually works when the man makes more money than the woman, which isn't always the case these days.

When I was in relationships with men who made more money than I did and wanted to be traditional, they paid for absolutely everything. I enjoyed being treated. In retrospect, however, I see that they could get bitter over this arrangement, especially if I was making a decent salary. The Bureau of Labor Statistics reports that nearly 50 percent of the workforce is currently women, so most men will assume you have some disposable income.[3]

When a woman is making a good salary, it's appropriate for her to occasionally offer to foot the bill, even if he refuses the offer. Unless he has clearly indicated that he doesn't want you ever to contribute financially, it's just a nice way to show him that you care and don't expect him to be a cash cow or sugar daddy.

Another option is to surprise him with tickets to a live event or movie as a gift. It's good to let him know that you aren't stingy and can be generous with your money and resources as well. He'll recognize that you'd be a thoughtful wife.

These days many couples eventually opt to share expenses because they both earn substantial incomes, or the woman earns more than the man. I originally had a hard time accepting this, because I thought it threatened my role as a woman in the relationship. I thought, "What next? Are you going to want to stay home with the kids?" When my now-husband asked me to pick up a tab on a date, I was so upset by it that I went to talk to the priest who later presided at our wedding.

The priest told me that he could relate to a man's desire to share tabs because he once dated a woman who made more than he did. He liked her but became resentful over how she always expected him to foot the bills. The financial burden was stressful for him because he was underpaid and overworked. He began to feel that she didn't care about him. After he told me this story, I realized that sharing tabs can really just be a way to make sure both daters remain debt-free and financially secure. That's not so threatening!

How Do You Know If You're Sharing Tabs?

If a guy wants to share tabs and you're the kind of woman who walks into dates assuming the man will pay, there will usually be a brief chat after a few dates. He might ask, "Is it OK if we split the bill?" Or, "Can we alternate who pays?" The discussion is typically very informal to spare everyone any discomfort.

Other women have said that they always take out their wallet before they know what the expectations are. If the guy is going to cover the bill, he'll state that or motion for you to put your wallet away. If not, you look independent and non-presumptuous.

Sometimes money comes up casually. One lawyer I dated said, "Girls think lawyers are all rich, but I'm strapped with student loans, so just so you know, I'm broke!" Other people are less forthcoming.

DATING WITHIN YOUR MEANS

Knowing a guy's financial situation can help you gauge his manners, motives, and fiscal discipline. For example, unless it's his "third place" (home is his first place, work is his second place, and a coffee shop where he spends a lot of his time might be his third place), a rich guy who takes you to a dive all of the time could be saying that he doesn't really want to be seen out on the town with you and doesn't value you enough to spend money on you. It's rude. If he has the money, and if he's trying to woo you, he should spend some—not a fortune, but enough to say he cares.

On the flip side, a guy who is deeply in debt and surprises you with something superexpensive might be showing you that you're a priority, but he could be destroying his ability to fund your future together. It's not impressive for anyone to outspend themselves all of the time. That's scary.

Jewelry shops frequently pressure men into emptying their savings account for an engagement ring, for instance, and imply that it's in poor taste not to. Make sure he knows that he doesn't have to undertake these feats of debt accumulation, and assure him that you will cherish a gift that's within his means.

Remember that a guy who spends lavishly may fit the sugar-daddy archetype mentioned earlier and expect something in return. Women should be wary of feeling that they owe a guy anything, so watch for these compromising situations.

Do Women Always Need to Date Men Who Earn More?

I used to believe that I had to marry a man who made more than me, so this applied to dating as well. It was the foundation for most traditional dating etiquette, so how could he not make more money? It was like the eleventh commandment.

A gal pal and I used to talk about this all the time. One night we were munching on some French fries in Chinatown and indoctrinating ourselves. We'd say, "I would never date a guy who didn't make more than me! He couldn't support the family! That's just a bad decision all around."

Both of us were well-educated and had good careers. We both grew up with stay-at-home mothers, and that is what we wanted for ourselves. We wanted to fight the changing tides and remain in our mother's worlds.

These days, though, it can come off as shortsighted and cold not to consider dating men who don't earn as much. According to the Pew Research Center, 22 percent of wives made more than their husbands in 2007, compared with only 4 percent in 1970.[4] Look at his ambition, career path, and long-term goals. Don't immediately eliminate a man because he's not quite at your salary level. We live in a society where men and women work side by side, have lucky breaks at different points, and may fall victim to a downsizing any time. Be reasonable.

Transportation

Etiquette regarding transportation depends on how well you know the guy. If you just connected online and it's your first time meeting him, it's better not to be picked up in his car. Meet in a neutral spot, and get yourself home alone if you don't want him to know where you live. It's actually considered polite for a man to let a woman retain some privacy on a first or second date, especially if you met online.

If you know him better, you can either meet him somewhere or have him pick you up. In the city I would often meet a guy someplace after work and have him walk me home. Cars were usually too inconvenient, although if he had one, he would usually drive me home.

Sometimes things get confusing with transportation etiquette. One guy caused waves with my male friends because he wanted me to meet him at a comedy club at night and take the subway home alone. A colleague said, "What? A man should secure a girl's way home, especially at night in a city with a high crime rate!" I think it depends on the city and the couple, but these issues mean that you need to decide how traditional you want to be and when you want to speak up. When I told Mr. Comedy Club that I didn't feel comfortable with my proposed journey home alone, his enthusiasm faded. So etiquette can be a deal breaker if one feels that the other's standards are too high.

There were other men who would drop me off at a subway station rather than drive me all the way home. Some people didn't think this was good etiquette and that it was a missed opportunity to talk more during the ride, but I wasn't always offended. It could be a way for him to save time, especially during the day. I would, however, expect to be driven home at night.

DOES HE RESPECT YOUR ETIQUETTE?
Some women need to coach men to follow their etiquette or personal preferences. Not every man is raised with an

appreciation for traditional etiquette, so if you have it and want him to abide by it, tell him that.

Let's say you want him to open doors for you. There are several things you can do. You can gently prompt him by pausing at a door before opening it. If he opens a door for you, thank him to reinforce the positive behavior. If he doesn't initially get it, don't make a huge issue of it during the first few dates; just go with the flow. If you start dating long-term though, tell him that you really like it when men open doors for you. The hope is that he'll start doing it.

If he still won't follow your etiquette when you drop hints, and you start to feel that he is being rude, you might want to take it on as a respect issue. You could say something like, "When you don't open doors for me, it makes me feel like you're not respecting me. I was raised to expect men to open doors, and I'd really appreciate it if you did that." It's a small thing, but if it means something to you, he should oblige.

Some guys will argue that opening a car door for a girl is a waste of time and calories because they need to go to the passenger side of the car. These things are up for discussion, but if something really rubs you the wrong way, it's better to politely raise the subject than to let it silently burn you up.

. . . .

Attilio: Women shouldn't expect a man to abide by every single one of their preferences. If they do they are looking for a servant, not a companion. If you can't reach a middle ground on etiquette, consider whether or not the relationship is worth it.

. . . .

PRETENDING YOU'RE BUSY AND PARTY-GOING

Some girls get the idea that they need to pretend they're busy so they don't appear desperate or as if they have nothing else to do. This can backfire. If a guy asks you out and you say you're busy after the second request, he'll assume that you're not interested in seeing him and are too shy or polite to say so. Play too hard to get, and guys will throw in the towel. If you truly are busy after two date requests, offer another date and time if you want to see him, to prove that you aren't blowing him off.

If you're at a party or group gathering, and there are two guys you like, the safest option is to be equally pleasant and polite to both. This way either could feel comfortable asking you for a date.

If you really want a date though, and neither has asked for one, you could observe them both, read the signals, and see who is more interested in you. Choose the more interested one, and ratchet up the flattery and flirtations to make a positive response more likely.

The wild card is jealousy. If you warm up to one of the guys, the other one could think, "Wait a minute, I wanted to date her!" and pursue you afterward.

WHAT IF HE FLIRTS WITH EVERY GIRL?

I always found it distasteful when a guy flirted outrageously with every attractive single female in his path. However, some men view this as putting eggs in many baskets. If you really like a guy who does this, make sure you get some face time. If you don't mind dating him along with five other women, accept a date request. If you don't like his ways, move on.

The concern with a guy like this is that maybe he likes flirting in general and won't stop even after he's committed. If you commit to a flirtatious type, watch out for that and speak up if you're ever bothered by his behavior.

A Heartbreaker Is Making the Rounds

After I split with a boyfriend, I found out that he had a bad reputation around town, and none of my friends who knew about him had warned me. I was angry and felt that someone should have told me. If a guy is a creep, girls should out him, right?

Here's the deal. Most people think it's fair that each person get to know someone on their own with a clean slate, regardless of his or her past. This is because different people click in unique ways, and people can learn from every failed relationship. In short, if you're dating him, most people won't readily discuss a guy's previous relationships with you.

I see pros and cons to this piece of etiquette. You probably shouldn't say anything to a girl if she's just starting out with a guy. However, if a problem crops up and you know it matches his previous bad behavior, then confirm, "Yes, he did the same thing to Chrissy." That way you aren't initiating any negativity but still helping the girl get insight into the guy she's with when she needs it.

The problem becomes more acute if you know a guy perpetually engages in behavior you disapprove of and seems to have a pattern. Isn't it right to warn friends? Is it worth the risk of angering the guy? Sometimes it is; it depends on the behavior and how strongly you feel about it. Are you so offended that you're willing to stand up for your views if there is backlash? It's hard to know where the line is, especially in a Christian community, so err on the side of caution, and try to be respectful.

. . . .

Attilio: If you're worried that a friend is walking into a battle-field, making her aware isn't a bad idea; just do it in a neutral sort of way. For example, "I heard something that concerns me, but I don't know if it's as bad as it sounds."

. . . .

chapter seven

GROWING OUTSIDE YOURSELF

If you come up empty year after year, is it really going to help if you keep doing the same thing over and over again? Stop trying to jam a circular puzzle piece into a square: The result is always unsatisfactory. Even if you're getting dates, there is still a problem if none of those relationships lead anywhere. The goal isn't to become a professional dater; it's to get married.

The famous actor John Barrymore said, "Happiness often sneaks through a door you didn't know you left open."[5] Many of us purposefully close most of the doors in our lives, thinking that if we just leave one door open, God will be forced to deliver a prince through that one and only door. It could be the "daily Mass-goer" door or the "makes over $100,000" door. When nobody comes through the door, we get bent out of shape and think, "Well, maybe I'm not supposed to be married." Maybe you need to open up some doors and windows and let a breeze in!

Remembering That Jesus Is a Roaming Shepherd

Remembering how Jesus works in general can help us understand how he works with us when we're dating. The Lord usually brings a conversion about through other people. As mentioned earlier, I'm a convert, and you might be surprised how the Good Shepherd reached out to me.

I was introduced to Christianity through a message board for a punk band, so I say, "I met Jesus online!" When I expressed my disapproval of a band member's rumored adultery on the road, a youth minister agreed and innocently asked if I was a Christian. I wasn't—but soon I was, based on our lengthy conversations. It was the equivalent of Jesus hanging out at a club after a concert, chatting with people in the audience and handing out business cards. Fast forward ten years later, and I'm well-versed in my faith.

If Jesus sees and knows everything and is capable of converting people online, he might also bring you a husband in an unusual way.

THE CHRISTIAN COCOON

When you're living in the secular world, it's difficult to live fully and confine your social interactions to religious and squeaky-clean environments. Yet that's exactly what some fervent believers try to do. After my conversion I thought I could avoid "backsliding" by surrounding myself with Christian people and only going to Christian events. I lived my life in a warm and fuzzy Christian cocoon of sorts.

Nevertheless, it seemed that some of the Christians in my upper-middle-class town went to church to keep up appearances rather than to grow spiritually. It was as if they acquired a church membership to go with their McMansions. The cocoon approach can curtail authentic spiritual growth by restricting our exposure to human suffering and broader social issues.

With the downsides that cocoons have, God may choose not to deliver one of these "cookie-cutter" men to you. You'll be forced to adapt and choose the best of the possible options.

It's important to remember that most people outside the Christian cocoon are not bad, clueless, or completely misguided. There are good people out there who may not be of your exact denomination or go to your same church but who really do have a relationship with God and share your core values. Some of them may blow you away with generosity and understanding, and you'll recognize the Lord in them.

Should You Only Date Other Christians, Catholics, Baptists…?

I dated a Catholic guy I met at a Protestant function on a college campus. Because he presented the Catholic faith to me in a positive way, I became Catholic myself. Had he chosen to ignore all non-Catholics and not date anyone who didn't agree with his views completely, I wouldn't have changed denominations.

I officially entered the Church after this relationship ended; my actions weren't to please the guy or out of some sense of obedience. I did it because I wanted to. Sharing your faith with others when appropriate can result in genuine conversions. While some people minimize these instances as "missionary dating," it's not fair to dismiss real soul-searching and sharing as shallow or misguided attempts to proselytize.

Sometimes a significant other won't follow your lead when it comes to religion, or vice versa. At those times consider if you can be patient with that person, accept his decision, and give him space to follow his path. The answer might be no. A friend of mine, Tim, was engaged to marry a woman he reconnected with after many years. She was heavily involved with her church of born-again Christians. Because he didn't want to immediately attend her church or become involved with their activities, she called off the wedding. As you can imagine, he felt that she was trying to force a conversion, that her love was conditional, and that she wanted him to conform to the expectations of her friends. This was an older couple, so child rearing wasn't at stake, but it was very painful for my friend to be rejected in this manner. He said, "I was initially very pleased that she had a spiritual life, but after that experience, I didn't want born-again anything. I felt those Christians were doctrinaire."

Be sure to explore a man's spirituality and disposition toward your church before getting engaged. You don't want to be the heartbreaker who pulls the rug out from under him, nor do you want to assume that a guy will accept your religion as his own without a discussion. However much you want a man to convert, it mustn't happen through force or manipulation. Remember that you're an ambassador of your faith; don't give him reasons not to convert based on your inconsiderate behavior. Even if you part ways, you don't want to be the reason a man negatively stereotypes Christians or religion in general.

LEAVING FEAR-BASED BEHAVIOR BEHIND

When I first started my career in the federal government, I was asked to go on a business trip to Reno, Nevada. Reno is like a microcosm of Las Vegas. I was nervous about the gambling and impropriety I would encounter there. Similarly, my boss was the daughter of a Lutheran minister and didn't think she'd be too fond of it either.

Much to our surprise, it wasn't that bad. You could play nickel slots for the same price it would cost you to go to an arcade. Since none of us had a gambling addiction or played with money we needed to use for necessities, nothing bad happened.

Nevertheless, there were two attendees who behaved as if the slot machines were going to jump off the floor and attack them. One of them wanted to find a way to attend the conference and not pass slot machines. This was a casino! There was no route without slot machines.

When you find yourself in dicey secular environments, remember that nobody can make you do anything that you don't want to do, and just because you have the opportunity to sin or do something regrettable doesn't mean you will. If your mind is in a positive place and you have a healthy sense of adventure, you will find goodness most places you go. Think like a victim though, and you could become one.

My husband occasionally goes to Las Vegas on business. I usually tag along, so we have been to "Sin City" multiple times. Recently I went to Caesar's Palace for a massage while my husband was at a conference. I told the massage therapist about this book. She said, "Oh! I'm a Christian dater, and I want to set up a conference for people who are dating online. I would love it if you would come and speak."

You might think that when you walk into a massive casino, you're the only person with spiritual underpinnings. It's not true. People want to hear the Christian perspective and to be inspired, even in a casino. Jesus meets people where they are and can work with anyone who is open.

When Nothing Clicks, Follow the Light of Human Virtue

I knew a priest who taught RCIA classes, and one night he asked the married couples why they married each other. They looked at him with clueless expressions. He said, "Yeah, it just happened, right?" He was referring to this invisible clicking action that happens between two people. Something needs to just *happen*. That's the life-giving spark that God injects into relationships. It's like the life force we all have within us that makes our hearts beat.

When nothing was clicking for me, this priest tried steering me in a different direction. He said to actively look for men outside my church environment. He said, "Just find a good guy!" As a friend told me, the perfect can be the enemy of the good.

When something isn't clicking, you know it. Make an adjustment! When things aren't gelling, God is usually saying, "Veer left," or, "Veer right." It's like being on the highway and choosing an exit.

If you find someone who doesn't share your faith or is unchurched, he should still be supportive of your religious practices.

When God Says No, It's Probably Time to Grow

If you're picky, do some analysis. I knew women who were traditional Catholics and wanted to marry a man who shared their own religious fervor, but when it came to the guys who were on the same religious page, they would say, "He's just not my type."

The choices are to grow in one of two directions: Accept a man who isn't a carbon copy of you religiously, or accept a man who isn't quite your type. Don't play a tug-of-war with God for twenty years and say, "No, I will only accept a man who meets these specifications." If God already said no for twenty years, he could keep saying no for another twenty, so sensitize yourself to the hints he sends. It may be that your path to holiness is to become more loving and accepting.

Bridging political divides. I initially thought I'd marry a Republican, so I dated politically. I even joined a dating site for conservatives.

A cute guy I worked with invited me to go to something sponsored by the Democratic Party. I wouldn't go. He sighed, "Ohhh, come on.... It's just softball!" And yet the guys I dated who shared my political views weren't always what I expected. One boyfriend was what people term a "GOP bad boy." He talked about his high standards but didn't walk the walk. It wasn't true that my party had a monopoly on morals.

My husband came along, leaning to the left like the Tower of Pisa. This upset me initially, but after much discussion, we are now both registered Independents. Sure, he might be more left-leaning and I more right-leaning, but we're able to peacefully coexist. We take pride in having grown together intellectually.

My parents don't always see eye-to-eye politically either but have been married for over thirty years. The trick is for each partner to retain personal freedom and a sense of identity in an environment of mutual respect amid the inevitable debates and disagreements.

You listen to what? I liked dating men who shared my musical tastes, but it didn't always happen.

One guy I dated liked Paul McCartney's solo music. I like the Beatles—I even toured their old neighborhoods in Liverpool—but Paul's solo work makes me change the radio station. I couldn't hide this fact from the guy and poked fun at him.

Unless the material is offensive, don't discount someone based on musical preferences alone. People will always have their own favorite band. Music and art should raise the soul and are a highly personal matter.

It's not often that I can acquire a taste for different types of music; I either like the sound or I don't. It's kind of like food; most people have favorite dishes. Disagreements about music and art are common, so if a guy is nice otherwise, give him space to listen to his own tunes.

There are ways for daters with differing tastes to show sympathy for the other's preferences. One guy I dated identified a new band that he thought I'd like. He loaned me a CD, and I loved it! Similarly, a man at work says that his wife joined his jam sessions not because the music was to her liking but because she wanted to spend time with him.

My husband has a palate for modern music. I think it sounds overproduced. He dismisses my music as being too guttural and passé. After much effort we discovered one or two bands that we both enjoy, and we've gone to their concerts. Those shows have helped fuse our musical sensibilities to an extent or at least provide some fond music memories.

Quit looking for a doppelganger. Even twins have differences. Even if you find a man who is a lot like you, you probably won't agree on every conceivable social issue, theological detail, music trend, diet, interior design choice, movie, TV show, or outfit. Get used to it. People are special because we are all unique.

Further, a couple might be two peas in a pod when they marry but slowly grow in different directions. I know a woman who married a man who was as religious as she, only to watch him change over the years into an atheist. Other people change in less extreme ways. These things cannot be predicted or antici-pated, so it's to your benefit to learn to live with people who aren't always on your wavelength.

RELATIONSHIPS TAKE WORK

A friend said, "I know someone who says that the right relation-ship shouldn't take work. That person is not in a relationship, because the minute anything happens, she's gone."

There were times when I wondered if I was trying too hard to make it work with my husband when we were dating. I learned not to be afraid of working on a partnership that has promise though. I used to chat with a man who was an Orthodox Jew from New York City, and he had valuable insights on dating and marriage. He said, "Anything worth having is going to take some work." He dispelled Hollywood notions of idyllic romances that last forever without some discomfort along the way. He had been married for years and had a large family, so his life situation lent credibility to his words.

Similarly, a coworker who had the benefit of wise grand-parents shared the same message. His grandparents had been married for many years, but he knew through his conversations with them that they didn't always click or view their spouse as their favorite person every day. Rather than get caught up in that, they embraced each other for life and let the daily irrita-tions roll off their backs. The big picture and the good moments were more important and worth preserving. Their patient mind-set and steadfast manner were the key to the success of their relationship.

I dated men with whom it should have been easy to form long-term alliances. We were on the same page in important ways, but they refused to work on anything or let foibles go. My husband's willingness to work on things and grow is one of the key assets that set him apart from the other guys and made him a keeper. Our differences weren't as important as our commitment to working together.

This bears saying because a lot of modern-day advice givers urge daters to avoid relationships that require work. Many articles, books, and speakers push this potentially self-absorbed and narcissistic philosophy. It's seductive when you're in a slump and read an article promoting this view, because it's appealing to think that you're entitled to happiness 24-7 and anything less is beneath you. By all means, if you're constantly feeling bad about yourself and having problems in a particular relationship, maybe you should back out. I have known women, however, who exaggerated problems in relationships because of a deeply held belief that the right relationship shouldn't require work and that their time was too valuable to invest fully in one that did.

DIVINE SIGNALS

Growing outside yourself doesn't mean growing away from God. When I was dating my husband and wondering if the relationship was right for me, I got a sign.

I went with him to New Jersey to meet his family for the first time. As I got out of the car at his grandparents' house, I saw a statue of St. Thérèse, my patron saint, on their lawn. Once inside the house I realized that his grandmother also had a strong devotion to St. Padre Pio, one of my favorite saints.

To me this was God's way of saying, "I know you're worried that this man isn't devout enough for you, but I am here with this family, and everything is going to be OK. This could work out if you want it to."

I realize that some people think it is foolish to look for signs, but my life is full of them, whether I look for them or not. It's a way that God communicates with me and reassures me. So if you get signs, pay attention, use discernment, and consider whether or not God is speaking to you through them.

chapter eight

THINGS TO CONSIDER BEFORE
COMMITTING

Before getting engaged, you absolutely need to discuss certain topics in depth. Don't assume anything. The saying that "to assume makes an ass out of you and me" is true.

Why doesn't everyone automatically discuss the important things? After leading many young couples through marriage preparation, one priest told me his theory. He said, "Some people want to get married so badly that they convince themselves that someone is 'the one' even when it's not so." People dance around crucial topics because they don't want any trifling details to delay or cast a shadow of doubt on their wedding plans. Highly emotional types can fall head over heels in love and be unable to see past their passion and delirium. Biological issues factor in too, as hormones start pumping in the interest of procreation. People can recklessly gloss over details in the heat of the moment.

Then there's the dangerous "God will take care of us" rationale. An article in *Crisis* magazine featured devout divorcees who candidly acknowledged that their marriages weren't bullet-proof.[6] They advised readers not to be lulled into a false sense of security or to think that their parish priest will always have the answer.

sion-making strategy. There should always be some wiggle room, but marriage is based on agreements and a commitment to the same vision.

. . . .

Attilio: Not every problem will be solved in a day, a month, or a year.

. . . .

VOCATION AND FINANCES

If the relationship seemed to be going somewhere, I always asked my dates point-blank if they had discerned religious life and if they were sure they wanted to be married. As mentioned before, this is a critical question in Catholic society. My directness added a measure of accountability if they ever broke my heart in favor of religious life and gave me some assurance that they were mature enough to manage their relationships responsibly.

What if he knows he is not called to the priesthood, but he feels called to do a great deal of charity work, teach theology, or take a job in the Church? These choices can mean meager earnings, so it's important to agree on priorities.

Know what your boyfriend earns and how much debt he has if the relationship is becoming serious. If the debt is substantial, talk to him about how he plans to pay it off. Can he sleep well with a lot of debt? If he's flippant and doesn't take his debt seriously, worry! However, if he's committed to paying it off and has a plan, relax. Either way, discussing existing debt is a good way of learning about his attitudes toward money and figuring out what kind of financial obstacles could be in your path. Also disclose your own earnings and your savings plan for retirement.

Remember that even if you date someone who is wealthy or debt-free, it doesn't mean that he will automatically be a good husband or always be well-off. Good financial management skills are a helpful indicator though.

OPENNESS TO CHILDREN

When we were in marriage prep, we sat next to a couple who couldn't agree about having children. The man was visually impaired and hesitant, but his fiancée was gung ho. They had obviously discussed children before. Perhaps the woman was counting on him to change his mind in marriage prep when the Catholic teachings about openness to life were explained. It didn't look as though he did.

He probably had concerns about having children because it can be hard to earn a good salary as a blind person. However, she had a right to have children. Since openness to children is a condition for a valid Catholic marriage and the vows state as much, this becomes a megaproblem for some. I could see they were distressed, but I wondered, "Why didn't they settle this earlier and avoid the anguish of getting so close to marriage before they came to agreement?"

Discuss openness to children in the first month or so of a relationship for sure. Don't do it on the first or second date if you sense that the man isn't ready for serious talk or would be scared away by it, but broach it early. It can be done casually. Just say, "When I have kids, I want to…". See how he responds and if he asks questions. He could say, "Oh yeah, me too! How many would you prefer?" You have your initial answer. It can be discussed more later if you stay together.

Some people have made a conscious decision not to have children, or they have a health problem that can cause infertility. If you are dating someone and figure this out, preferably within the first month or two, you can address the issue before you introduce him to family and have a ring. If you cannot agree on a path forward, you can move on before becoming too deeply invested in the relationship.

Usually though, the issue is timing and readiness, which is a gray area. I knew one couple who divorced partly because the man wasn't ready to have children when the woman was. He didn't feel ready to support a family yet. The woman left him, married another man, and immediately began having children. The man remarried and had a child as well. They both ended up as parents, just with different spouses. I can't help but wonder if having a better game plan starting out would have helped them stay married to each other.

· ·

Attilio: God's will has a lot to do with when a new life comes into the world, so no amount of planning for the right moment will serve as a guarantee. But if both husband and wife are not at least considering the same time line, the tension between them can bleed into every aspect of their life together.

· ·

CHILD REARING AND EDUCATION

Based on the way you and your boyfriend were raised, you will probably have different opinions about the best way to raise and educate a child. It's not necessary to make firm decisions about everything before marriage, especially because some child-rearing methods depend on the temperament and talents of individual children, but at least establish that your partner is open to your concerns and thoughts and willing to compromise when necessary.

Talk about your attitudes toward schooling and day care. These topics can elicit strong reactions from would-be parents and can have significant economic consequences. You don't want to end up with someone who completely opposes your convictions and causes you to have a crisis of conscience over dedicating resources to the well-being of your child.

Past Marriages and Children

If your boyfriend has had previous marriages, ask him why they ended. Knowing the cause of failed marriages should help you keep a future marriage intact and walk into it with your eyes wide open. Make sure he has learned from his mistakes and is committed to making a future marriage work. A popular statistic says that 67 percent of second marriages and 74 percent of third marriages fail, so it's vital that you know what you're getting into.[7] Similarly, if you had a previous marriage, it will be helpful to a boyfriend if you explain why the marriage failed, what you learned from it, and what you will do in the future to strengthen a subsequent union.

I typically ruled out men who had been previously married. I knew the stats weren't on their side, and when I spoke to them about why their marriages had failed, I was so saddened by the responses that I worried about their relationship skills overall. I realize, however, that some people end up with an abusive or controlling spouse, and they have few options. Maybe his ex lied to him about something important. It's possible that he just had really bad luck during his first marriage and he is capable of creating a stable second marriage. If you genuinely like him, give him a chance to prove himself.

Be sure, of course, that a previous marriage has been properly dissolved and that you are both free to marry. For instance, Catholics have an annulment process that can take time to complete, and it is not a given that an annulment will be granted. Until it is, the person is married. You want to be above reproach, and dating a man who is still married isn't right. What if he changes his mind and goes back to his wife? What if she is still trying to work things out?

Second marriages shouldn't be treated as second best. I have met people who minimize second weddings purposely, saying, "Oh, I've been married before." If you want your friends and family to respect your second union as much as the first, and if you believe in the relationship, show everyone that you take it seriously.

If you or your boyfriend have children from a prior union, you need to discuss how they will be raised and what the custody agreement is. This includes revealing if you had a child and gave him or her up for adoption. It used to be that adoptions could be kept secret, but so many parents and adopted children feel the need to reconnect that it's prudent to be open about it with a prospective spouse.

Children and Church

When I worked at a craft store, I once watched a mother help her son pick out items for a project that had something to do with confirmation. The father was wandering around the store, and when he met up with her, she quipped, "I'm not even the

Catholic; why don't *you* help him?" Her voice was resentful.

That was an example of the type of conflicts that can develop when couples don't share the same faith. If you and yours share the same faith and have similar church attendance, celebrate! Your life will certainly be easier. If not, set some expectations before marriage on church attendance and how children will be raised. If one spouse is Catholic and the couple are married in the Catholic Church, the children are required to be raised Catholic. The Catholic parent should take the lead with regard to religious education.

FAMILY COMPATIBILITY

Visualize your families gathered together at your wedding. Does the picture make sense? Do you like his parents and think you could accept them as in-laws, and vice versa?

Traditionally it's important to click with the family of a pro-spective spouse. My husband was old-school Italian about this. He purposely left me alone with his family at times to see if I could build a connection with them. Afterward he triumphantly declared, "They love you!" While this made me nervous, I think it was for the best, because I developed affection for his relatives. I can also leave my husband with my family and have confidence that there will be a steady flow of conversation.

Couples should be concerned about family harmony for many good reasons. If a parent becomes seriously ill or needs help after retirement, adult children may need to chip in. If there is strife to begin with, this becomes more stressful. Also consider the nightmare stories of overbearing parents interfering unfairly in the relationships of their married children. It's considered the kiss of death to marry into a family where one or both parents

dislike you with a passion. Such pitfalls may be more important for women to consider, especially since most women change
their last name to match their husbands', and the woman and
her children usually tend to morph into the husband's family
slightly more than he will blend into hers.

Yet knowing the value of pleasant relationships doesn't cancel out the reality of parent-child conflict and dysfunction. So
although the traditional recipe for marital happiness includes
happy relationships with your in-laws, you ought to take that
with a grain of salt and heaping tablespoon of charity.

I thought, too, that some people I met in the Christian community were overly concerned about pedigree and that they
unfairly judged people by the successes and failures of their
relatives. Yes, we inherit some things from our families, and yes,
children of intact families are more likely to stay married themselves. But every individual makes his or her own choices.

The truth is that few people grew up in families that were
like a 1950s TV show. Some people have been abandoned by
their parents, have experienced ugly divorces, or must keep one
or both parents at arm's length because of toxic personality traits.
While singles tend not to wear these realities on their sleeve on
a first date, these issues may be part of their stories. It doesn't
mean that someone won't make a good spouse. Family weirdness
isn't really all that unusual, after all. Where is it on the scale? Can
you live with it? Will your relationship work out regardless?

How Does He Handle Emergencies?

An emergency is one of the best ways to determine if your boyfriend really can embrace your family as his own and remain
trustworthy through thick and thin. Unfortunately, statistics

show that while a wife will typically buckle down and care for a sick husband, a man is six times more likely to leave a wife who develops a serious disease such as cancer or multiple sclerosis.[8] How your boyfriend handles medical emergencies and illnesses in particular is an important indicator of his character.

There was a medical emergency in my family as we were getting ready to visit my husband's family for Thanksgiving. Although we were not married yet, he decided to stay local with me for my family's sake and relayed the message to his folks. It was handled very smoothly, which allowed me to focus on the emergency. That kind of synergy is what you want.

Another time I needed immediate medical attention in the middle of a rainstorm. I had only dated my husband for a few months at that point, but he ventured out in the downpour to drive me to a doctor after-hours. This was someone who would be able to support me through illnesses or a difficult pregnancy.

A friend of mine, Amanda, who is married to a very good man, Eddie, told me stories about her husband's prize-winning responses to her father's illness. One weekend Eddie drove to see Amanda for a date, only to find that her father had suffered a setback and was in the hospital. Rather than getting upset, he joined Amanda with her family at the hospital, and they hung out in the cafeteria.

This sensitivity translated well into the marriage. Once married, her father's illness worsened. When he was on his death-bed in the hospital, Eddie had a friend drive him to the hospital during his lunch break, and he whispered to his father-in-law that it was OK for him to leave and that he would take care of Amanda.

Do your best to find a man who remembers the significance of the relationship during emergencies. When you marry a man, he becomes family. My husband said that when I walked down the aisle, it was the last time he saw me as being separate. The wedding made me part of his family.

Relocations, Traveling, and Stress

Are you dating someone who might relocate, take business trips, or deploy? If he doesn't volunteer the information, ask the question. It's important to know where you will be living if he will be absent for long periods of time, and if you can handle it.

I dated a man who swore that girls were immediately turned off by relocation talk. This frustrated him because, like many men, he thought he might like to relocate at some point in his career, and he wanted to be transparent about that with women. If you find the love of your life, it may not be as bad as you think to spend a few years in another location. Look for the silver lining, and try not to categorically reject a guy just because he might move out of the local vicinity at some point for family or career. If you don't like the idea of moving permanently, try to negotiate for shorter-term moves and inquire about moving at times that are more beneficial to you.

Many singles go through deployments during the dating period because of military conflicts overseas. Some couples choose to remain together during deployments to test the strength of their relationship, and others break up permanently or temporarily. Deployments (or long trips) can be a good "final exam" before a proposal.

Not everyone will be happy with a traveling man. The stress and loneliness can drive women nuts. It's better to be honest than to crack under the pressure. Try to use opportunities during the dating period to test your resilience and independence if you aren't sure that the lifestyle is for you. Some people learn to use time apart for personal development and take a class or start a new hobby.

Modern-day scenarios include the woman as the business traveler or the one whose military assignment requires deployment, or both the man and woman having demanding schedules. Whatever the case, proactively create balance. One of you should try to land a stable job so that there is some consistency to daily life. In my case I worked in a chaotic job where I could have been asked to support disaster relief efforts. Before my wedding I found a more predictable job elsewhere.

DAILY DETAILS: HEALTH INSURANCE, DIET, AND CHORES

Do your jobs have health-care coverage, and if not, what will you do to get it? Health care is important for a secure family life and could save you money in the long run.

Assess each other's dietary requirements and determine how to manage them. A vegan friend of mine said that diet can be more important than religion when dating! It's increasingly common these days for women to adhere to strict diets that prohibit the intake of dairy or meat products. Men aren't as likely to go for strict diets without a doctor's order, but I have met men with severe food allergies.

If one of you is on a diet, how are meals at home going to work? Will you be able to find meals to satisfy both of you, or will you prepare two distinct dishes? Will you share the responsibility, or will that belong to one person only?

Chores cause many arguments! Early on you might as well get some idea of how the two of you will handle this area. Unless you won't be working outside the home, I'd recommend making sure that your potential fiancé will share chores in marriage. You can divide them up later. Just get a commitment from him to contribute. If you don't, he could try to weasel out of everything, leaving you with the bulk of the labor. Women still do most of the housework, which can be unfair if both husband and wife are working full-time, so request equity up front.[9]

MEDICAL HISTORY AND FERTILITY

Talk about diseases that you've been exposed to and long-term illnesses that require management. If you need medical tests for a health concern, have them. Additionally, if anything like heart disease, diabetes, addiction, breast cancer, or other serious illness with a genetic component runs in your family, disclose it. Even if you don't personally suffer from the problem, these illnesses could develop later or predispose your children to health problems.

Women need to be honest about their age and the impact it has on their fertility. Some couples choose to cut engagements in half because they want children and understand that a woman's age could hinder her ability to get pregnant.

PORNOGRAPHY ADDICTION

For Christian women the idea of porn being present in their marriage is alarming and dehumanizing. It's a huge letdown, and it means that the house may never be truly kid-safe.

I listened in disbelief as a speaker at our marriage preparation class explained that she knew Christian families who were being torn apart by porn addictions. In one case she said that a friend didn't feel comfortable leaving her house to hang out with girlfriends or attend church activities because she knew her husband would go porn-crazy in her absence.

Tell your boyfriend that you disapprove of porn. If he's on the fence about it, your disapproval could coax him to kick it from his life. Guys might lie about porn, but knowing that you disapprove could bring him around. A male friend of mine was engaged before he finally told his fiancée that he had a porn addiction. He was a regular churchgoer and even counseled for an organization to help women recover from abortion. He asked his fiancée for forgiveness, and she supported him. To break the chains of addiction, he smashed his home computer! Other men might benefit from professional help or a twelve-step program when trying to break this horrible addiction.

It's not true that every man views pornography as a birthright, so don't settle for someone who insists on keeping this damaging habit and denies the harm it does to you and your marriage. There are men who think it's distasteful and damaging to society, and they choose to live a more cerebral and centered life. Find one of those men to marry, because porn is poisonous.

PREMARITAL COUNSELING

Premarital counseling helps to ensure that you're really ready to get married. Some ministers and priests recommend it in conjunction with church-sponsored marriage prep and view it as routine. Others believe that counseling prior to marriage is a waste of time and even a red flag, so you may get some flak from close friends and family if you go.

I heard a grandfatherly church leader say that the fragility of today's relationships startled him. He reminisced, "When I was younger, and there was an argument between two people, they worked it out." According to his recollection, it wasn't as common for two people to simply explode on each other, fade into the crowd, and never speak again. He thought our interpersonal skills took a collective nosedive starting about fifty years ago. I guess that's why more people are signing up for premarital counseling; many of us need brush-up classes in basic friendship.

Additionally, our current relational climate means that a lot of people suffer multiple heartbreaks before marrying, and they come into marriage with baggage and hang-ups. Some couples need a referee when they broach important topics, or they need help overcoming bad behavior patterns. Being willing to attend couples counseling can be a sign that two people value a relationship enough to make sure it's built on a steady foundation. Staying together or breaking up are choices, and going to counseling is usually one resoundingly good choice to work things out. It won't guarantee that problems will resolve themselves or that the relationship will work, but it shows a mutual commitment that can help couples weather future ups and downs.

At the same time, if you need a referee to resolve every area of your relationship, you have to wonder if you can afford the relationship! Maybe you need to date someone who is more agreeable, or perhaps you need to become easier to get along with. Health insurance doesn't always cover couples counseling, but a lot of people say the investment is worth it. Charitable organizations offer free or low-cost counseling, and some Christian counselors have sliding rates.

During our Pre-Cana marriage prep program, one of the speakers mentioned making a pact with her husband to immediately go to counseling if either felt it was needed. While their plan may not work for everyone, committing to resolve issues promptly is a worthy goal.

COMPATIBILITY

How compatible are you as a couple? Does everything flow like a gentle stream, or is it more of a rocky ride? What do you love about him? What could you do without? If you see bumps in the road, make an honest assessment of how much you can adjust and still be happy, and if you find the status quo acceptable.

Some couples are more naturally compatible than others. Traits that bring you together can also drive you apart, depending on the situation. For instance, my husband and I both have fiery Mediterranean temperaments and type A personalities. We can butt heads, but it also means we understand each other. We've gotten to know what our quirks are. If you can deal with your mate's quirks by joking, you're probably in good shape.

Everyone needs to adjust a little, because there are no made-to-order fiancés. Many divorces, however, are chalked up to compatibility issues or "irreconcilable differences." If the gap between you is too large and bridging it requires constant attention, or if you're both always accusing each other of failings and shortcomings, it may be best to move on before it's too late.

chapter nine

WHEN HOLY ROLLERS DON'T MEASURE UP

I remember going to a party soon after my heart had been broken by a church usher I had been dating. I couldn't believe that someone who was so into church life had treated me so poorly; I was scandalized.

At the party I met a girl who was fashionable and seemed to have it all together. When I told her my story and how stunned I was that some Catholic boys were so hurtful, hypocritical, and hardly virtuous, she looked at me and said, "Oh, Amy, you didn't know?" No, I didn't! When I became a Christian, I thought I was entering a special society of honest, upright, and noble people, or at least a community with the same goal of goodness.

Initially I took the high road and regarded moral failings as exceptions to the rule. I let things roll off my back and returned to the same roller coaster. Then I learned not to be so idealistic. After a few years of repeat performances, I realized that these disappointments weren't quite exceptions. The majority of my wide-eyed girlfriends had the same horror stories, which overlapped both in theme and in minute details.

There are men who hide behind the cross, finding comfort there. They tend to be more isolated, living in the shadows where normal flaws turn into glaring problems. They might not get the proper attention or the socialization needed to ripen them into maturity or prepare them for the demands of relationships with women. If their faith community doesn't take a holistic approach to spiritual development, they may not have the principles you think they do. In a close romantic relationship, cracks in a person's personality and spirituality will become evident.

Some of these guys might actually mature into good spouses one day, but at this point they are more like fruit that has not ripened enough to buy and take home with you. When a fruit is picked too early, you don't know if it will eventually ripen, if it will stop short of ripening, or whether it will taste good once it ripens.

THE QUEST FOR MINISTERS AND SEMINARY DROPOUTS
During most of my dating years, I hung out with lovers of Christ. Girls in the Protestant world wanted to marry someone in the ministry, and the Catholic girls wanted the seminary dropouts. They thought this was the best way to get a strong Christian husband. Not every devout Catholic woman can or should marry men who are former seminarians though!

Even if you succeed in finding the coveted man of the Word, be sure to get to know him as a person, and be careful about making sweeping generalizations. One time I was giving tours at a government agency where I worked, and a man on the tour asked me for a date afterward. He was a former minister and disgruntled with God. The pressure of everyone coming to him for answers had made him snap. He was divorced, and even though he might have known the Bible, he was not a faith-filled person by the time I met him. He didn't even like talking about God.

THREE ARCHETYPES TO AVOID

I met enough religious men with troublesome tendencies to develop three archetypes to avoid: "The Dream Weaver," "Mr. Smokey," and "The Dabbler." Some guys are mixed, perhaps 80 percent Weaver plus 20 percent Dabbler. This is my armchair psychologist's version of a temperament test where people are usually not purely of one category or the other, although they have dominant tendencies. To save yourself grief, you will want to be able to pick out men displaying these archetypical behaviors.

The Dream Weaver
• is hypersensitive;
• can be opinionated;
• has lots of burned bridges;
• seems "off" or makes you feel like you're walking on eggshells;
• suffers from a mental illness or is periodically unstable;
• lives in an alternate reality;
• exhibits vocational confusion.

Example: I met a man in a Christian environment who made a good first impression. Soon after meeting him I got sucked into his version of reality, which wasn't always balanced or healthy.

I thought his concepts of career and money were way off, but somehow I believed that everything would work out. When he began arguments and lost friends, I dismissed it as youthful enthusiasm on his part.

He eventually told me that he had a mental illness and also, later, that he stopped taking his medication. I noticed behavioral changes. He abruptly broke up with me without providing an understandable explanation. He also said he wanted to become a priest. Because his vocational change was so sudden, many people were concerned about him.

Regardless of words of caution and advice from many in his life, I believe he remained firmly in the grip of his delusions. Although someone with a mental illness would find it difficult to get into a seminary, that didn't stop him from marching forward, even if the path led nowhere.

I eventually cut ties because I couldn't justify wasting my time and emotion on someone who was living in another reality. The stress caused me deep suffering, and there had to be an end to the insanity if I was going to lead a normal life.

Last I heard, he's still publicly claiming that he's discerning religious life but reports no progress on the matter!

How to handle a Dream Weaver: Remain firmly rooted in reality and be true to yourself. Nurture your own emotional stability, and keep your goals in mind. Get some history on the guy, if you can. Remain plugged into your family base and your community, and be receptive to the comments they offer on your relationship and plans. Resist the urge to run off with him in a Romeo-and-Juliet moment. You could regret it.

These guys might not be bad people, but delusions and instability are big problems. When he charms you with his talents or Jesus-speak, remember that those things alone will not make him a good marriage partner.

Mr. Smokey (derived from "Smoke and Mirrors")
• always puts his best foot forward;
• displays lack of integrity and moral compass;
• seems phony;
• acts narcissistic;

- will be deceptive;
- is smart.

Examples: One Mr. Smokey I heard about hopped between relationships with women and seminaries. Perpetually causing offense on both fronts, life seemed to just get more complicated for this guy at every turn. Yet he always found ways of getting people to trust him and help him along. His evasive ways looked smoky to me, and it was revealed that he also suffered from some psychological problems, which added a Dream-Weaver component to the cocktail of dysfunction.

I dated a Mr. Smokey who strategically dated one girl from each of several different social pools, so that he could concurrently date lots of Catholic girls without their knowing it. This was in a small town, in a small community, so what he did was truly an accomplishment in the art of deception. When I busted him, he said, "Oh, I'm such a jerk." I thought, "Well, if you knew you were being a jerk, why did you do it in the first place?" But since he was a Mr. Smokey, smoke and mirrors were just his way, and he couldn't explain the *why* except to say that he was putting eggs in lots of baskets and treating dates like job interviews.

Besides everything else, both of these men were verbal supporters of chastity, but their speech didn't translate into their behavior.

How to handle a Mr. Smokey: This is the hardest type to handle, because these men are so deceptive. They prey on Christian women's sympathies and their inherent desire to trust someone who appears to be religious. I think they are the most manipulative of the three types and the most culpable for their actions.

Mr. Smokey relies on your dismissing red flags as "little things," so keep track of them. When something doesn't feel right, ask him about it. Tell him how his smoky ways make you feel. Shine a flashlight on questionable behavior, so it can't go on for a long time unchecked.

The Dabbler
- seems to be a good and upstanding individual;
- easily gains your trust;
- can come from a privileged background;
- is commitment-phobic;
- is indecisive;
- may be older than most of the guys you meet in your scene.

Examples: I watched an acquaintance walk through the door to join a book talk. She looked dazed. What could have happened? Maybe somebody had died, or maybe she just received some other terrible news. She seemed to half-listen to conversations going on around her. She must have come in an attempt to stop focusing on the train wreck that replayed itself in her head.

After we became closer friends, she told me she had met a man online, and he had relocated to be closer to her. He was educated, professional, and a man of faith. After some time he said that he was ready to propose. Nothing could have made her more happy and excited. Before he proposed he went on a retreat. She thought he wanted to spiritually prepare for the big question he was about to pop. She couldn't have been more wrong.

Expecting to hear a proposal, she was stunned when instead he told her that he was going to discern religious life and felt his next step might be seminary. The man had probed this question before, although nothing he had told his girlfriend led her to believe that the case was still open or that he would revisit it.

A year later he had not pursued religious life and was with another woman, which he flaunted to his ex. What happened here? His behavior seemed to have a component of commitment-phobia. It didn't matter what or who it was, he couldn't settle down. He was always on to the next adrenaline rush, the next new turn of events.

Epic letdowns can happen at the hands of Dabblers, some of them the result of questionable spiritual guidance. I interviewed the coordinator of a young adult church group for an article I was writing for the *Washington Times* in 2008. She complained about seminarians being encouraged to date, even when they were discerning a vocation that requires them to discontinue romantic ties. She said, "Some priests told the men to go date. It's not fair to women, who are more emotionally invested in the relationship. Their expectations are different, so stay away from the collar."[10]

How to handle Dabblers: If you correctly diagnose a Dabbler early on, the safest bet is to keep your distance. Seriously dating him is like gambling. If there are signs that he might be about to quit dabbling, you could give him a little bit of time if you aren't as risk-averse as I am, but be ready to move on if he can't commit after a few months.

I know one married couple who dated while the man attended seminary. He eventually chose her, but it doesn't always happen that way, so don't take anything for granted.

These men can seem like very good people, so it's easy to want them to stick around after the breakup. They might be so knowledgeable about the faith that you think, "He's such a good person to know." Be careful about remaining close friends though, because your heart could still flutter.

THE MATURITY TEST

In order to get better at spotting negative behavior patterns in men, I read *Safe People* by Dr. Henry Cloud and Dr. John Townsend. The book advised avoiding people who seem less mature than their years, education, or background would suggest, because you are more likely to be hurt in relationships with them.[11]

All of the men I met in these three categories displayed that warning sign loud and clear, so if learning my archetypes is too much of a bother, just look out for men who are inconsiderate of others and who do not happily accept adult responsibilities. Some of the more attractive ones will come off as conceited, as if their dating prowess is more important than investing in long-term commitments and earning someone's trust. For differing reasons they fail to deal with their cold feet, resolve their indecisiveness, or choose from the available options and stick with one path.

IS THERE HOPE OF REHABILITATION?

If you meet a guy who is religious but also dysfunctional or disconnected, can he change? Yes, but it will be a result of a personal epiphany, and it probably won't happen on your timetable. You might be able to encourage the epiphany and be part of it, but you can't force it. It will seem like his faith should save him, but if he has underlying issues, he may not hear God's message, or he could just have a long road ahead of him.

The Florence Nightingale Effect refers to a situation in which a caregiver develops a romantic attraction to her patient, and a boyfriend is not your patient. You might feel that you know him better than anyone else and know exactly what issues he needs to deal with in order to heal, but you can't deliver him from most of these problems without being brought down yourself in the process. If he is drowning, you can try to help him, but if you begin to go down with him, your priority should be to save yourself.

Even the most patient, long-suffering women eventually need to abandon men who say they love Christ but who nevertheless lack good relationship skills.

BEWARE OF POACHERS

Guys dating in the Christian scene already know what you're looking for. It makes sense that they might emphasize their "churchiness" to you. Problem is, if they know what to say to get a date, how much does it mean? Is it an act?

Guys who enter the church scene solely to get dates are sometimes called poachers because they're like wolves picking off sheep. They size up their prey before making an attack.

Ask a few questions to find out if a guy is a poacher. Is he a member of a church? Does he know any of the priests or ministers by name? Be careful not to confuse a poacher with someone who is new in town or has just gone through a conversion. A poacher is new to the church scene because his primary purpose is meeting women.

I met a poacher at a church function, and it turned out that he lived on the other side of the country. After some e-mails, I realized that he might never step inside a church again. He was simply looking for cute girls.

RIGHTEOUS INDIGNATION

When a man who claims to be above average in religious observance and morals dupes you, it's normal to be extra-angry and to feel humiliated. When a man uses religion to earn your trust only to turn around and mistreat you, it can amount to spiritual abuse. Victims go through more than a normal breakup when spiritual abuse is in the mix. Betrayal can cause them to question their religion, the trustworthiness of their clergy and fellow-believers, and even God.

Some women will report tragedies to clergy and get apathetic responses. I personally reported a phony to a vocations director and got a "my hands are tied" response. I think it's an injustice when valid concerns from mistreated women are swept under the rug, but it happens for a variety of reasons. Take care of yourself first in these circumstances, and move on to greener pastures. The more you try to communicate and are rebuffed, the more upset and hysterical you'll get, which can be used to discredit your concerns.

At the same time, share your experiences with people who are willing to listen and learn from them. These scenarios are more common than some people think, and wrongs that are kept under lock and key can never be addressed.

. . . chapter ten . . .

FIGHTING FOR RESPECT AND CHASTITY

Nobody can make you do something you don't want to do. An episode of the Discovery Channel's *MythBusters* showed that even a professional hypnotist couldn't make people do anything that was against their moral fiber.[12]

It's important to know what you want and don't want before a date and how much control you really have over your actions. One night I learned that even with a little too much wine, I didn't lose touch with my core convictions.

WHAT PART OF *NO* DOESN'T HE UNDERSTAND?

I once dated a man who was attractive and had a knack for making me laugh. Let's call him Mike.

Mike seemed familiar with the virtues required to lead a Christian lifestyle and professed that he wanted a chaste relationship with me.

On one occasion he treated me to a fancy dinner, and we ended up having too much to drink. Unfortunately, I felt that he used the situation to his advantage.

I had some cards stacked against me. I was young, inexperienced, naïve, and apt to follow his lead. I liked him a lot and feared damaging the relationship by being disagreeable. Additionally, as we all know, wine can have an adverse effect on people.

Since it was late and he had had a lot to drink, we didn't think he should drive home. What to do? I didn't want him to be a drunk-driving statistic, but I wasn't going to have him stay in my place either. That would spell trouble. He agreed to find a hotel room.

Once I was at home, safely tucked into my bed, he called me repeatedly and tried to get me to return. I said, "No. I really don't think that's appropriate." Again he called. "Oh, come on, come back over and stay with me." Again I said no. No matter how tipsy I was that night, I wasn't going to compromise my convictions and do something I would regret, no matter how hard he tried to make an indiscretion happen. I talked to him about it the following day, but his denial resulted in an unproductive conversation.

Since I felt strong enough not to cave in to his drunken antics, I didn't immediately end the relationship. I gave him the benefit of the doubt. Unfortunately, Mike didn't just have a blind spot with chastity when we were together. He had other issues that made it difficult for me to maintain a good relationship with him. I had to break up with him.

Later I saw Mike around town. I was surprised when he approached me and thanked me. I learned that he was reading self-help books and doing some serious introspection.

Sometimes the Lord is relying on us women to have a spine. If we don't tell the guy no, who will? In a close relationship the deepest part of a person, the most wounded part, can come out. You may be the only person who gets to glimpse the vulnerable spirit in that man.

This was a difficult experience for me. Saying no was hard, because I really wanted it to work with him. But I wasn't willing to let my principles collapse or to be spiritually derailed. If I stayed with Mike, everything of importance to me, including my relationship with Christ and my free will, would have needed to be forcefully shoved aside. It just wasn't worth it.

WHEN HE SAYS HE WANTS TO BE CHASTE BUT ACTUALLY DOESN'T

Another boyfriend I had said he believed in chastity, and he went to all of the right Christian events to convince me he was sincere. Regardless, he was always finding a way to isolate me and create an opportunity for us to fail. One time he was very bold, and I spoke up: "Ummm,... I really don't want to do those things, and I didn't think you did either." Silence ensued. There was no apology. The expression on his face said, "Busted!"

Some men I met, no matter what they told me, would try to leverage private moments to their physical advantage. This was frustrating, because I wanted to believe what they said, which was that they weren't interested in premarital sex.

If a guy is a repeat offender, don't pretend to believe his lies. You can let him go with steely resolve, but be sure he understands why—that it's not just the physical land mines that disturb you but his misrepresenting himself. Can you trust someone who says he's someone he's not? If he's apologetic try to work with him, but don't be fooled if his behavior doesn't improve.

IS IT OK TO BE ALONE WITH HIM?

People might say that it's never good to be alone with a guy you're dating, because human weakness might prevail over good intentions. They'll tell you not to stay in the car for long, go to a hotel, or let him in your apartment. These are logical precautions, and they will eliminate some uncomfortable situations. These tactics aren't foolproof though.

A guy who really wants to make a move will do things in less private situations too, such as secluded park benches and parking garages. This can cause embarrassment and high-school-like humiliation, so it really isn't always as simple as staying out and about in public places. You need to monitor the temperature pretty consistently and speak up if necessary to break the spell of the moment.

Alone time can be risky, but sometimes I wonder if we've made it unnecessarily so. I've noticed this: Some men who are always in group situations might not learn to control themselves alone in close quarters with a woman they like. The minute they're in a room with her, away from people—*bam!*—they attempt to get some forbidden fruit. I always found this disturbing, because although I knew to avoid too much time alone with a guy, I thought I had a right to expect decent and respectful behavior in any situation. So my challenge to everyone who is pro-chastity is, don't treat alone time like a crime—thinking that way can bring out the worst in people. You can emphasize group or public activities for the right reasons without unfairly demonizing alone time.

A guy needs to spend some private time with his girlfriend. In fact, there are some conversations that are not for public consumption. From much experience in restaurants, I know that discussing some personal topics when dining out can feel inappropriate and uncomfortable, both for the talkers and the other diners nearby. Telephone and e-mail are options, but communication experts agree that these forms of communication are inferior to face time.

Shoot for Ideals, Avoid Extremism

Ideals help us shape our relationship goals and lead us in the best direction possible. However, taken too far, idealism can lead to relationship obstacles and extremism.

The focus on chastity in the Christian community has led some women down a road of puritanical behavior. It's not all their fault, because they have been persuaded by the advice of people with lofty credentials whom they respect.

Having been a puritanical dater myself, I can say from personal experience that I don't think completely eliminating physical contact works for most men and women who are trying to find a spouse. There should be some form of bonding, because dating foreshadows marriage, and a man is unlikely to propose if he isn't confident that a physical connection is there. This is different from cultivating an expectation of promiscuous behavior. Little things that couples do when they are together show that they have affection for one another: hugs, kisses, hand-holding, cuddling. Women are typically not as reliant on physical affection as men. We shouldn't give men everything they want, but don't be surprised if a guy gets offended if you won't hold hands or ever show any form of endearment.

While we are used to hearing about how oversexed the world is, being too restrained can also bring trouble. St. Thérèse's parents, Blessed Zélie and Louis Martin, lived as brother and sister at the beginning of their marriage. They had to be strongly encouraged to consummate the union and to fully embrace their calling. It didn't come naturally.

Avoiding signs of affection can also keep you single forever. If you absolutely cannot handle any physical affection, you should consider why that is the case and what that means for your life direction.

THE FIRST KISS

The most ethically astute people I met insisted that it wasn't wise to kiss before you were in an exclusive relationship. A kiss signifies "going steady." I came to agree with that assessment and even found that some dating gurus and psychologists who write for the secular scene consider that reasonable advice. Why become bonded to a person when you aren't sure about the relationship? You open yourself up to a heartbreak that could easily be avoided by simply holding off for a few weeks. Kissing too early raises the stakes too fast. Face it: It'll hurt more if things go south and you've smooched someone. A lot more!

WHEN YOU FAIL TO LIVE UP TO EXPECTATIONS

Even couples committed to chastity make mistakes. It's part of life. We're not perfect, and to be human is to have weaknesses. Many devout couples confess premarital transgressions even though their intentions were initially admirable.

What if you've failed to live chastely, but you're with a decent guy who is attracted to you and wants to marry you? If he's serious and the relationship is a good one, let him propose or move toward the wedding date. Not every misstep means that a relationship should be trashed.

Other times a guy isn't serious, and he is just using you. If it becomes clear that a guy's primary interest is physical, there's no point in continuing with him. Even if you feel loved, it isn't love if he's only involved for flesh.

After a failure, making amends with God through the sacrament of confession and prayer can be a healing balm. Even after you make your peace though, there might be a lingering suspicion that God is judging you or withholding forgiveness. Let's face it: Things don't always end well. What if the guy turned out to be a player and you feel robbed of your virtue and self-worth? What if you get pregnant? One lapse can change your whole life. You can be haunted by regret.

The best thing you can do is to get back on the right track and persevere. Don't waste time cutting yourself down after a mistake. Hope and faith can bring healing to any situation. Positive action offers more promise than wallowing in despair or self-pity. God truly is love and doesn't abandon people because they don't always live up to expectations.

GOD DOESN'T ASK YOU TO BE A DOORMAT

I used to think God was OK with my being a doormat. By selectively reading Scripture and historical applications of it, I thought men always called the shots. I stopped myself from expressing differing views and developing my own opinions, because I was afraid of emasculating men or being a "feminazi."

The results were devastating. For one thing, I wasn't respecting myself as a creation of God in my own right. If Jesus had given me my own mission in life, I didn't know it, because I was too absorbed by the men I dated! I was looking to make *his* mission my mission. It's fine to look for someone with whom you can share a purpose, but don't completely lose your identity in a man. If he disrespects you, you could end up making excuses for him or going into denial because turning against him would be the same as turning against yourself.

My misguided attitude ruined relationships. I thought that if I wasn't any trouble for a guy, he would like me more. But when I wasn't true to myself, the men subconsciously knew it, and some of them took advantage of me because they could get away with it.

One guy, for example, started our relationship by treating me like royalty, but he ended it by treating me like yesterday's fad. One time he said under his breath, "My mom would never put up with that." He didn't say it in reference to me—it was in regard to someone we knew—but I wondered if he didn't have me in mind. Apparently his mother had clear boundaries, and the family knew it. She commanded respect.

A man once told me about a famous musician's relationship and how he mistreated his ex-wife. I saw the man as the villain, but he painted the woman as weak—because she tolerated it.

Really good guys will treat women well without any prodding. True integrity shows in what you do when nobody is looking, so a woman's lack of self-respect is no excuse for a man's abusive behavior. To keep a healthy balance in a relationship, women need to stick up for themselves. Being steamrolled a little bit can quickly turn into a lot. Maintaining balance can be as simple as saying, "Since you chose the last two restaurants we went to, I'd like to choose this time." That comfort level will translate into bigger things, such as finances. "I paid off my credit card balances and student loan, so before you buy that big TV, I'd feel better if you told me about your own debt repayment plan." Years ago that last example would have horrified me. Now it's not a big deal.

As a recovering doormat, I can tell you that when you change your tune to be more self-respecting, the guys who don't treat you well will either not be attracted to you or improve their manners in order to get along with you.

chapter eleven

COPING WITH DISAPPOINTMENT AND BETRAYAL

When relationships end, or you haven't had a serious dating relationship in a long time and loneliness becomes too heavy a burden to bear, you can feel that your life is a mess. Chances are that you've either experienced this feeling or watched someone else go through it.

I always found it hard to move on from unanticipated letdowns, and I watched friends struggle as well. Recovery can be a slow and purposeful uphill battle punctuated by deep thought and prayer. Sometimes people get ribbed over taking breakups hard, but broken hearts are no laughing matter.

DISAPPOINTMENT AND DEATH

One minister I spoke to believed that a loss of a relationship could feel like a death, so it's fitting to mourn when relationships end. Since each person is so distinct and special, an ex is irreplaceable. If you have to see your ex regularly or watch him marry a friend, closure can be hard to achieve. The sadness can be long-lasting, and wounds might be reopened repeatedly.

In fact, heavy emotional stress results in physiological changes that can be difficult for the body to recover from. I had a relative who reportedly died of heartbreak after her husband fled during wartime. I also pass a row of graves each day that remind me of the compounding effect that misery can bring. My aunt lost her boyfriend to a drug overdose. Seven months later she died of the same cause. Two months later her father died the same way. A few more months, and the boyfriend's father died. Now they lie side by side. Their depression was contagious and spread like a deadly virus. For this reason it's important to make a priority of recovering from disappointments and breakups.

DO REALLY BAD HEARTBREAKS EVER HEAL COMPLETELY?

When one of my friends got married, I was nursing a recently broken heart. My friend had suffered some betrayals before he met his wife. I wistfully asked him if the despair went away when he got married.

Much to my surprise he said, "I love my wife and am excited that we're married, but there are some scars that never go away. A part of me still hurts when I think of my ex." This was someone who knew that he was going to marry his wife after meeting her for the first time, so the relationship was as storybook as they come.

Although the reality of long-term scars wasn't what I wanted to hear, my husband and I both agree with his assessment. If you're moving toward a committed relationship and still harbor pain from a previous boyfriend, don't lose hope. Keep putting one foot in front of the other. The pain may never go away, but it will diminish over time. Having old hurts does not mean that your current relationship is defective either.

· ·

Attilio: Don't expect a guy to forget his past loves, especially if
he's not the one who ended the relationship. If you are
together for a while, stories of the past should be looked
at like that: stories. Obviously, the man is now with you,
and he cares greatly for you. Otherwise he wouldn't
allow you to know about a vulnerable point of his life.

· ·

THERAPY

Therapy can help when things are bleak. But is it always necessary? No, and yet spiritual directors frequently recommend it.
They usually aren't trained to do in-depth counseling and can't
always relate to the emotional roller coasters women are on after
a breakup.

Therapy isn't effective for everyone, however, and not all disappointments call for that kind of an investment. One question
can help combat therapy mania. Do your problems fall within
the realm of normal breakups and anxieties about getting married? A few weeks, maybe months, of sorrow or confusion are
expected. Maybe you can beat the blues yourself and become
stronger for it. With that said, there are times when therapy can
be exceptionally useful for recovery and well-being.

Therapy was in vogue when I was dating. By the time I got
married, I had seen so many therapists for breakup-related crises
that I had difficulty remembering their names or keeping them
straight. I thought I should start charging my boyfriends a fee,
because each relationship was costing me thousands of dollars.

When I interviewed for a job that required a security clearance, I needed to explain the purpose of my therapy and autho-
rize the release of all medical records for review. Those advisors

who had suggested therapy quickly had not been knowledgeable about the security clearance process and the residual stigma that counseling has in some professions. That experience made me realize that it's up to you to filter all suggestions wisely, to remain cognizant of your career requirements, and to keep your medical records manageable.

When to discontinue therapy. Some therapists don't signal when sessions should end, and patients have difficulty figuring out when to discontinue treatment.

Reevaluate ongoing therapy when you start to think, "Wait a minute,...why am I going to this appointment? What was my homework again?" If you aren't even plugged in, what's the benefit? Maybe you and the therapist can agree to go to an "as needed" appointment schedule.

If you argue with the therapist regularly and the relationship becomes adversarial, it probably isn't a good match. Patients do best with therapists with whom they share core values and a basic human understanding. It's best to make changes if you aren't clicking, because you pay whether it works or not.

Therapy junkies. Some people go to therapy "just because." If you want to go for an extra helping hand but don't really need it, objectively evaluate whether you can afford it. Therapy has benefits, but it's also a for-profit service industry. Most therapists initially tell you that they want to see you improve and move on. But I have seen a lot of people develop dependencies that therapists are inclined to feed, becoming "friends" with the patient partly because they want their paycheck.

I think most of my therapy sessions were a waste of time and money, but I went to therapy because I didn't have enough good friends of my own to talk to. When lines get blurred, remember that as long as you're paying, your therapist is treating you. It's not a true friendship and shouldn't be regarded as one. A trusted friend may be more helpful in times of need, because she is caring about you, not treating you.

Also, what man is going to want to marry a therapy junkie? That could be a five-hundred-dollar-a-month habit that he will need to worry about, along with having a therapist he will need to impress. Lonely single women can grow overdependent on a therapist, and it's something to be wary of.

MOVING ON

Moving on can be hard to do when you wish that your previous relationship had worked out, but there is more joy in moving forward than remaining locked in the past. Remember what it felt like to have butterflies in your stomach before a date, and resolve to recapture that excitement in your life.

Changing scenery and creating a sense of movement helped me change gears and move beyond breakups. Local places can prompt old memories in the weeks following a split, so do some traveling, visit friends out of town, commit to charity work, take a class, or make some day trips to provide yourself with distractions. After one breakup I traveled to Britain to fulfill a lifelong dream, reflect, and snap out of my melancholy. It also gave me something upbeat to talk about for a few weeks! Of course, be responsible and don't accumulate a debt that will be hard to pay off, because that will serve as an unwanted reminder of your heartache in the months ahead. The changing seasons, new music, and flipping pages of my pocket calendar helped me move on too.

Eventually I disposed of things that reminded me of past flames and deleted e-mails and contact information to make room for someone new. Purging removed the temptation to reread old e-mails or contact an ex. Not everyone can stomach a purging like that though. My husband prefers to keep old correspondence, because he wants a complete record of his life.

Entering a new relationship can be scary and riddled with doubts and false starts. Even if I knew my ex didn't want to make amends, I always worried that I was dating again too soon, even months after a breakup. My hesitation was caused by a nagging suspicion that things could work out if I tried harder, but this was never the case. Letting go of that need for a happy ending felt like losing a battle, but hanging on out of misplaced loyalty or inflated idealism is pointless. When you have recovered enough that you don't need to talk about your breakup incessantly, you can probably date again. God provided guideposts to encourage me onward, and I trust that he will for you too.

I mentioned a trip to Great Britain following a breakup. Upon my return the Lord sent me an Anglophile, and we bonded over British music and culture. On our first date he said, "I know this teacher who had cancer, and her husband left her. Can you believe that? What a jerk!" My previous boyfriend (John from chapter one) detached when I was very ill, so this comment was uncanny. For me that was a signal from God that other people could relate to my experiences and that it was OK to open up, trust, and find someone else. Not everyone was going to treat me as my ex did, and all men deserve a clean slate.

Setbacks happen though. I was with another guy two seasons later, walked into an event, and recognized my ex. I felt uncomfortable and left. Did that mean I wasn't ready to date again? I don't think so—it's just trial and error. Don't let the occasional bump hold you back or discourage you from moving forward. It's important to persevere and swim through the flashbacks until the coast is clear.

When Is It Too Late to Turn Back?

What if your ex comes back when you have already started to date someone else? When it's really love and the person makes amends, you can turn back even if you're involved with someone else. But usually the breakup occurred for good reason, so it's not that simple. Problems don't just disappear. Don't recommit unless you're sure that things could succeed and old problems have been addressed. A reconciliation shouldn't occur out of loneliness or neediness. It's also risky to try to resurrect a friendship too soon or needlessly continue a conflict by blowing off steam. Reopening wounds and continuing to let your ex upset you can make a breakup seem like a science project. It can also give the guy a perverse sense of satisfaction that he really got your goat.

When my husband and I started to date, we were both still getting over our exes. The week after we started seeing each other, both exes stirred up old passions. My husband's ex pursued him for a few months with letters and e-mails. He resisted because, although he had cared for her, the issue that caused the breakup didn't disappear. Her efforts to make amends weren't sweeping enough to convince him to try again. He saw a relationship with me as more promising.

My ex was less persistent. After months of silence he e-mailed me birthday wishes. There was nothing of substance in the e-mail, so I decided to ignore him and move on. I certainly second-guessed myself, but my decision to ignore him provided closure and an opportunity to start fresh. His e-mail was too little too late.

BEWARE OF HYPERSENSITIVITY

One trait I see a lot in unhappily single women is hypersensitivity and an inability to let things roll off their backs. I realize, however, that women who have been through repeated disappointments and betrayals might cultivate their sensitivity in order to sniff out relationship problems early. I can relate to this!

At one time I was too trusting and didn't seem to catch on when people were up to no good. Then I went through a phase in which I looked at my relationships under a microscope and asked for second opinions a lot. This may be OK, but where do you stop? Where is the line between requesting good counsel and improving oneself, and paranoia? Overcompensating won't improve matters.

Hypersensitive people will blow small conflicts out of proportion and not know how to smooth things over. If they often make big deals over small misunderstandings, others will feel as if they're walking on eggshells. Soon the hypersensitive people are drags to be around because they're constantly taking offense.

Guys might say you are damaged goods or have too much baggage if everything is a problem. Even if you manage to get through the dating and engagement period with raw nerves, it won't make marriage easy. Thin skin makes for relationship hell.

Are you hypersensitive? You might already know, since it can be so unpleasant! One telltale sign: Other people often become confused, impatient, or dismissive when you complain about something or say that you're hurt. While many of us were raised with the "It's OK to express your feelings" and "No feeling is wrong" concept, this won't be helpful if you're hypersensitive. Use your analytical faculties and minimize your emotional responses to determine what's a legitimate hurt and what is frivolous. Good friends could help you out, but you need to be willing to suffer the sting if they dismiss one of your concerns.

It will be easier for you to find happiness if you learn the "water off a duck's back" approach when sensitivities threaten to lead you astray.

. . . chapter twelve . . .

SECULAR SISTERHOOD

The "secular sisterhood" is what I call the growing club of Christian women who feel called to marriage but who nevertheless remain single for long periods of time. While singleness has benefits such as absolute freedom and never regretting a commitment mistake, these women might burn with frustration because their lives don't progress in the way they expected. As they advance in age, it's less likely that a vocation will take form. As they get older they may think they have more to lose and less to gain by making a commitment.

Many things go into the creation of a secular sister. Sometimes a woman says that she just can't find the right one or that it's increasingly difficult to find a man who supports chaste dating. This can seem like a satisfactory explanation, but I typically find that it's incomplete and perhaps lacking in self-awareness. Other contributing factors can include self-sabotage, a lack of grounded guidance from mentors, and a rapidly changing culture that confuses women of a traditional Christian mind-set. Negative thinking and behavior are also culprits, as well as simply not making marriage a goal and priority.

The good news is that it's relatively easy to break out of the secular sisterhood if a woman recognizes that she's in a self-defeating rut and wants to escape to greener pastures.

RECOGNIZING SELF-SABOTAGE

The majority of professional African-American women are single. Author and actor Hill Harper spoke to CNN about his book, *The Conversation*. Harper interviewed single African-American women for his book and reported that some repeated the mantra, "I can't find a good man." Harper says those women attract what they say in their mantra. However, he also met women who thought there were lots of good guys out there. Their "positive and open spirit" tended to attract good men and make relationships possible![13]

In the Christian community some of our most devout, talented women believe they'll never find a man who is good enough for them or who meets their standards. Rather than finding ways to compromise, making their expectations more realistic, or more willingly finding the good in others, they dig their heels in. These same women may also blame self-induced problems on others rather than addressing their own propensity to block opportunities.

A popular form of self-sabotage in Christian circles is for single women to lead a nun-like existence that is inappropriate for someone seeking marriage. They might become so focused on fine points of theology that any potential suitor would need to be standing footsteps from a monastery or seminary door to please them. This attitude sets these women up for repeated disappointments. You can see why I coined the term "secular sisterhood" to describe this peculiar limbo.

Leading a timid church-mouse life can seem like a safe approach in religious environments, but in reality it can be an avoidance pattern. When church mice encounter frustrations or disappointments in the dating scene, they may passively decide to remain single rather than feel imperfect or take a risk that they fear, in their hyper-piety, might lead them to sin. Taking the easy way out can be tempting, but remember that fear, unaddressed weaknesses, and murky life goals can delay marriage (and life fulfillment) indefinitely. A life with hardly any commitments or resounding successes is like a car running in neutral. You won't get anywhere.

There are many ways to hold oneself back, so breaking out of self-sabotage can mean different things to different people. Always, though, it means making changes—even if they are minor tweaks—and having a courageous attitude. It means looking in the mirror and being brutally honest with yourself. What do you need to do in order to get what you want in life? Something about you needs to change. What is it?

Conversing regularly with trusted mentors and friends can help enhance your self-awareness and maybe show you a different way to live. Listen to differing views and advice, because you are looking for ways to improve. For example, a male colleague encouraged me to consider dressing differently when I was in my early twenties. I wore lots of black and apparently wasn't making the best impression. He said, "Amy, you look good in black, but you also look good in colors." So I tried harder to select colors when I shopped. Then he noticed that I was choosing only blues and purples, and so he said, "Try some warm colors. Everything you wear looks cold!" He helped me adjust my outer appearance to reflect my inner self. It sounds like a minor adjustment, but it took conscious effort and friendly support. The result? Once people didn't need to look past the drab clothing, they noticed my true personality faster.

If you tend to be negative, find a more positive group of friends. Weed out people who bring you down. If your friends criticize men nonstop, gossip, make excuses for their unhappiness, and don't take the initiative, you will no longer fit in when your walk becomes more empowered and creative. Sometimes you need to change scenes in order to take the next big step in life.

ADVICE TO TAKE WITH A GRAIN OF SALT

Not all advice is created equal, and some can actually keep you single for longer, so carefully evaluate words of counsel before absorbing them into your dating strategy. I knew women who embraced one or two lines of advice like gospel, and it hurt more than helped.

Some people say, "Just pray more, and it will be all better." I've tried this, and it won't magically guarantee the outcome you seek every time. When I sensed that a breakup was imminent, I spent a day on a mini-retreat, praying for things to improve. When I got back in touch with my boyfriend, he was still a jerk! My running away from the problem might have made it worse. God listens and answers prayer, but prayers are not meant to help you control others. You could hear something in prayer that steers you in the right direction, and the Lord may answer you in a profound way, but good relationships require more than a superior prayer life.

Other people advise, "Don't ever settle for a man who is not exactly what you dreamed of, even if you're getting up there in age." There are some things you shouldn't settle for—don't get me wrong—but you won't ever find Mr. Perfect, because he doesn't exist. Also, some expectations probably should change with age. I am told that the landscape changes for singles in their late thirties, forties, and beyond, because it gets harder to find never-married men. While it's OK to rule out previously married men when you are in your twenties, you could sabotage your chances if you continue that mind-set twenty years later.

Secular sisters might justify their perfectionism by saying, "We're all called to be saints." True, everyone should strive to be the best possible person and have a meaningful relationship with God. But don't assess everyone against a St. Francis of Assisi. Don't expect most men to be like ideal priests or ministers.

Also, ignore advice that urges women to expect men to practically worship them. While a man should love, honor, and respect you, he probably won't let you have your way every time.

HAVING HELP

When women are young, attractive, and have everything going for them, they may forget that nobody can be an island unto themselves. Everyone needs a helper sometimes. Guys who lift weights might ask a friend to "spot" for them. Similarly, women sometimes need help doing routine things.

Single women used to be able to rely on their families and community to assist when issues arose, but not so much these days. Communities aren't as tightly knit, families are spread out, and people are frantically busy.

Consider the practical consequences of not having a spouse when you're making relationship decisions. Remaining single comes with an inconvenience charge. If you make choices that keep you single, be prepared for the added expense of hired help.

The people who helped you when you were growing up may not always be around.

Coveting Engagement Rings

When I was unhappily single and on the secular sisterhood train of thought, I always seemed to notice women's engagement rings when I was on the subway. I felt like the only one without a ring. It started to bother me and make me feel self-conscious, perhaps unloved. At one point I thought I would purchase a ring to remind me of God's love.

I chose one that was the shape of a crown. I thought it had lovely symbolism, because I thought of Christ as a king, and me as a princess in his kingdom. My intention was to wear it on my ring finger on my left hand. A guy said, "No, don't do that; you'll never get a proposal." Fortuitously, the ring was out of stock, and it never arrived in the mail.

If you want to marry, don't wear a ring on your wedding finger. When you do that you send a strong message that you're not interested in men. When I didn't wear a ring, I got plenty of dates. The minute I got engaged, nobody pursued me. That ring is like a red traffic light.

You may want to flash a stop signal and become temporarily invisible to men who are looking for a wife. *Not looking* is a short-term mood or state of mind though, and using a *permanently taken* sign could cause embarrassment. If you remove the ring, the question may be, "When did you get divorced?" Married people can become upset when their spouse neglects to wear a wedding band. It's a form of miscommunication, and so is wearing a ring when you're not married.

NOT APPRECIATING THE ONE YOU HAVE

One reason why a woman remains single is that she doesn't appreciate the man she has in front of her and can't rise to the occasion when it's time to commit.

I knew a girl who was engaged to a guy who treated her well. She eventually decided she wasn't happy enough and broke off the engagement. A few therapy sessions later, she realized that she just had a case of cold feet. She really loved her fiancé and wanted to get married.

Unfortunately for her, it no longer mattered. She may have resolved her issues, but the guy was crushed. He wouldn't marry her after the rejection. I would have preferred to see him so in love with her that he said, "It's OK, darling; I understand that you had a phase or mood swing." Instead he backed away and firmly maintained, "This is a huge decision and a major commitment. If you aren't sure, I can't marry you."

It was her turn to be crushed. The guy dated a mutual friend and became engaged within a few months. His new fiancée was ecstatic. Nevertheless I overheard a few people wondering if he had made a mistake not working on the first relationship.

To our surprise the original girlfriend wasn't angry with her ex, and she wouldn't indulge any second-guessing. She instead confessed that she had blundered by not appreciating the man she had. In her opinion it could take years to meet another man of his integrity, and she regretted her actions.

While it's not uncommon to have cold feet or to be unsure about something, don't lose sight of the good you have in front of you until it's too late.

Accounting for Your Time

If you are beautiful, successful, and have been single for a long time, be prepared to give men an account of how you've spent your time and why you're still uncommitted. They want to know, and it's actually for their own self-protection.

Once you get into your late thirties, for instance, there is probably a reason that you're still single. What went wrong in your previous relationships? What are you doing to prevent the same thing from happening again? These questions may sound prying and nosy, but in reality men who ask these questions are trying to make sure that a relationship with you has promise. He doesn't want a broken heart, and he doesn't want to be with a woman who is careless in her dealings with others.

At the end of our first date, my husband blurted out, "So why are you still single?" I was shocked, but what he meant was, "You seem so cute, together, and successful . . . and you should be snagged by now. What's the deal?" I told a horror story or two and said that I had difficulty finding a guy who was long-term commitment material. You should have an explanation too, although you shouldn't recite it like a carefully practiced alibi, which will make people wonder what you're hiding. Just be honest, share a bit of your history, and express optimism for your future.

Stay Positive and Resilient

If you're tired of being in a rut and want to get married, maintain a positive mind-set, spring back from failures, and know that happiness is the best revenge if you've been hurt by previous boyfriends. Avoid self-pity and excuses. Make the time to go out, and keep your appearance top-notch. Actively pursue marriage rather than assuming it will just happen. The reward for your efforts might just be a good relationship and engagement.

. . . chapter thirteen . . .

ENGAGEMENT!

I thought engagement would be the smoothest part of the relationship, but I found that it can be a very stressful time and that not every couple makes it through the test. Even couples who have made sensible decisions and constructed a good plan should be on the lookout for unexpected disruptions and anxieties.

How Long to Wait for a Marriage Proposal

One priest told me not to date a guy for more than two years without a proposal. From what he observed via marriage preparation, the likelihood of getting a proposal went down after two years. He felt that a man should know if his girlfriend was "the one" after two years, and if he didn't propose by that time, something wasn't right and probably never would be. It might not always be true, and I'm not sure that one size fits all, but there is no shame in managing your time.

I decided to follow his advice—it had the ring of truth—thereby establishing a time limit on how long I would date a man before moving on. I decided to walk after two years, no matter how much I loved a boyfriend. Attilio found this upsetting. "What if I'm not ready? Why won't you wait for me?" Other people told me, "Never force a man to propose." I wasn't forcing anyone to do anything. I was being firm about the value of my time. Cultural shifts have made it more acceptable for men to drag their feet for three, four, five years, which can be unfair to women's biological clocks. Being resolute about the value of your time and drawing a line in the sand might be something to consider if you're concerned about a man taking you on a wild goose chase.

Regardless of the old-fashioned advice I took, some good guys take years to propose. That is my disclaimer and reality check to you. These guys will baffle others because they don't fit the bad-boy image, and onlookers will make excuses for them, such as, "Oh, that's Irish men for you…".

One way to tell if a guy is going to come around or not is his behavior. The good guys I have seen who dragged their feet didn't ever seem disinterested or ambivalent toward their girlfriend or her family. They consistently gave signals that they were committed and not planning to go away. These were the men who were very involved with their girlfriend's lives. The truth was that they were planning their big marriage proposal but weren't ready to do it yet because they were agonizing over details, financial readiness, and their ability to take on family responsibilities.

The guys who string you along will probably be insincere and have an inability to remain optimistic during low points in relationships. Some guys just aren't mature enough to handle commitment, and these are the ones who, without warning, will make an excuse and break up with you just when things seem promising.

WAITING FOR HIM TO POP THE QUESTION

In our dreams we might imagine a guy popping the question exactly at the right moment. In reality, waiting for a guy to propose is torturous for a lot of women. I remember one girlfriend telling me that she woke up every morning wondering if it was "the day." She analyzed each day to predict the likelihood of the big question coming or not. She'd think, "He's going to be working late tonight, so it couldn't be this evening." This constant anxiety can drive the most well-adjusted, faith-filled woman bonkers. The anticipation is unbelievable, and it's common to get uptight.

Most women know the proposal is coming based on private discussions with their boyfriend. Men usually won't propose out of the blue. Some won't even initiate a frank discussion about it until they drop a few well-received hints. They test the waters with signals, questions, and anything else that will give them a good indication of whether you will say yes. They do their research beforehand, because the thought of your saying no terrifies them.

If you want to speed up a proposal, keep an eye out for his hints, and be encouraging. Smile, gaze into his eyes with excitement and joy, go ahead and talk about what your ideal ring would look like. Discuss hypothetical scenarios, and let the conversation meander into future plans.

You might want him to slow down. If you stay shy or a bit reserved, he will. Of course, there will be opportunities to talk openly about timelines, but the subtleties usually come first.

THE LENGTH OF YOUR ENGAGEMENT

The timeline pressure these days is for couples to get to know each other for a year or two before engagement. When my parents were young, one year was more common, but when I was engaged, two years was the rule of thumb. If a couple got engaged before the two-year mark, they'd usually be encouraged to have a longer engagement. For example, if a couple got engaged after dating each other for a year and approached a priest for marriage preparation, there was a good chance that the priest would support a wedding date that was a full year out. At the same time I noticed that if a couple was in their thirties, well-educated, and in good standing with their parish and clergy, they might be able to move forward more quickly, while a younger couple would be questioned more carefully.

It seemed like recommended time lines kept getting longer, and it didn't always *feel* right. Most girls I know got impatient and insecure after about a year of dating a man (or sooner!). The long wait could feel forced, especially if everything was going well and there was no real reason to delay a marriage. Some clergy who preach chastity can be especially demanding about couples waiting a standard amount of time before getting married though. The inherent problem is that longer timelines tend to increase the risk of veering off the chaste path.

When couples who view chastity as their top priority buckle to outside pressure and wait too long to get married, impurity sneaks in, and they are saddled with guilt or a pregnancy. They suffer for living their lives for others. If you and your fiancé are mature and serious about chastity, consider getting to the altar quickly. Rest assured that some people in the "two-year mandate" universe will lecture you or question your sanity.

On the flip side there are other things to consider besides chastity when it comes to time lines. For instance, urgency to get married based on sexual attraction alone can mean that other important topics aren't discussed. Speedy courtships and engagements are risky if there haven't been enough opportunities to see every side of someone's personality or to become acquainted with family dynamics.

Both short and long engagements can prompt a flood of questions from others, so either way, be prepared. Both time lines raise separate concerns, and Christian couples may be pulled in opposite directions. You can't please everyone. It's up to you and your fiancé to examine your own hearts, read the stats on marriage and divorce, and use common sense. For instance, some stats I read when I was dating said that college-educated people in their mid- to late twenties fared better in marriage than less educated people in their early twenties. Based on that information and the fact that it can be harder to complete degree programs when you have a family to tend to, some people elect to finish a degree before getting married. My husband received his master's degree days before our wedding.

Nobody can tell you exactly how long to be engaged or when to get married, but I've noticed that couples typically prioritize either the chastity issue or getting to know each other thoroughly. Both are important, and it can be hard to get an A+ at both, especially when there are naysayers on both sides of the aisle, urging you to sacrifice one at the expense of another.

COHABITATION HURTS NEGOTIATING POWER

According to the University of Denver, 70 percent of couples cohabitate before marriage these days.[14] While that stat translates into a society where *non*-cohabitating couples are seen as unusual, they are the ones who are smarter. Stats also confirm that couples who embrace cohabitation before marriage are more likely to get divorced. Casually mention this to anyone who tries to tell you that cohabitation is a prerequisite to marriage.

Both my husband and I were (and still are) dead set against cohabitation. Most people I met who fell into the cohabitation scenario did it out of laziness ("I'm too tired to go home") and a false sense of economy. Also, when you're deeply in love, it can be hard to tear yourselves apart. Sometimes marriage is seen as taking too long to get lined up because families have high expectations for the wedding. Others are seduced into believing that they need to live with a person to get to know him or her, disregarding the fact that people are people, not clothes to be tried on and discarded.

Don't allow the pride of some pro-cohabiting couples to sway you. Remember that some people who themselves cohabitate will secretly admire your strength for living independently. For instance, a nonreligious male colleague praised me for my decision. He said that although he and his wife had cohabitated and he saw it as being the standard choice for engaged people, he didn't want his own daughter to follow in his footsteps!

Since marriage has elements in common with a contract, your negotiating power is severely compromised when you cohabitate because you can't quickly withdraw. When you're dating, for instance, you can say, "I can't marry you if you don't get your finances under control." If you live separately you can disappear for an evening or weekend to show you are seriously thinking about things. That can scare a guy into a much-needed change or intellectual growth spurt. Your absence will speak volumes and force an honest discussion. You lose that bargaining chip when you live with him before marriage because then 1) he can take you for granted, and 2) you want peace in your living quarters, so you won't be as willing to demand changes. You're more often forced to settle for the status quo, and the guy is less likely to fight for you because he feels he has already won you.

Another hidden "con" exists with cohabitation. If you've failed to live chastely and now you want to get married, living separately allows you the opportunity to recover from lapses in discretion. During marriage prep a priest will probably ask if you are sexually active. If you say yes the priest or minister might ask you to abstain for a few months leading up to the wedding, to regain some of your virtue and also show respect for the guidelines of the Church. If you are already living separately, this is simple. If you live together it's a problem. What if the priest goes on to say, "Oh no, I can't preside over this wedding if you are cohabitating." Then you will have to disrupt your living situation and go through all kinds of chaos in addition to the normal engagement growing pains, just so you can move back in together in a few months.

War Brides

Wartime can interrupt courtships and postpone engagements. Older generations expected couples to wed hurriedly before deployments. A boss told me how her first husband deployed after they had a rushed wedding—and never came back. Based on fears and a desire to prove a commitment, some people rush weddings before deployments or during home visits. I suppose that when you're in love, you'd rather be a widow than never be married to your "one" at all.

Today's younger generation faces different circumstances though. In the old days wartime communication was limited, and women didn't always have careers. Marriage was an important financial safety net and assurance that the bond would survive the long period of sparse communication. Now communication is easier, and single women can usually support themselves. There aren't as many benefits to quick decisions.

Guys increasingly want to test a woman's loyalty through deployments too. They have learned that some women, married or not, cannot take the pressure of deployments and abandon them when they're overseas. "Dear John" letters are always dreaded, and nowadays a deployed woman might get a "Dear Jane" letter too.

A deployment was what my husband needed before deciding he wanted to marry me. Initially he wasn't sure that remaining together during a six-month deployment was the best option, but I wanted to stay committed. My loyalty prompted him to propose when he got home. This is a typical pattern these days, but I won't pretend it's easy. I had to say no to a few guys who wanted dates during his absence, and I worried about missed opportunities.

Deployment-induced delays can be torturous, but the risks of hurried weddings in wartime are many. Even if your guy comes back in one piece, the readjustment period can be hard. He may have fallen prey to posttraumatic stress and not be the same person you fell in love with. At the least you will look different to each other after you have been apart for a long time, and it takes effort to reconnect.

Because war brings themes of life and death so close to the surface, gut feelings come into play when making decisions. The pressure and risk factors can force serious discussions earlier in a relationship than anticipated.

If you want to stay with a guy who's deploying, recognize that time lines may change. You'll need to be flexible in your marriage anyway, and an early deployment is great practice in flexibility and discernment.

If you're thinking of going into the military yourself or have already signed up, your wedding and family life may end up being nontraditional. The military can make some choices for you and impose bans on having relationships with military personnel you serve with. I remember choosing not to join the military when I was single because I had a vision for my relationships and domestic life that couldn't coexist with military duties. Nevertheless, joining the military right out of high school is how many people find success in life, so if that's you, have the best engagement and wedding you can under the circumstances.

IS IT NORMAL TO FREAK OUT?

People freak out all of the time during engagement. They wonder if they're marrying the right person, if they can stand their in-laws, if they can work through their problems, if they will be able to have alone time, and so forth. When all of these concerns hit a person at one time, along with other stressors such as work, college, and social commitments, people can lose it. You are not abnormal for having an anxiety attack in a stressful situation. It's how you handle your panic that matters.

I melted down when my husband proposed because I had convinced myself the night before that he wasn't going to do it. He had just returned from deployment and was scrambling to get my ring back from family in New Jersey (unbeknownst to me), and the time that elapsed was enough that I ran out of patience. When he finally proposed I was so stunned that I could hardly respond. For a week or two, I was very quiet and didn't even tell my parents that I was engaged.

I contacted a married friend of mine, Ann, to ask her what she thought about my odd response. It turned out that I e-mailed her on the same day that her husband had proposed to her twenty-some years earlier, and she had been a basket case as well. She told me, "I so wanted Bob to propose!" But when he did she actually got physically ill! Ann is one of the most stable and levelheaded women I know, and she has a great partnership with her husband, so she really was making a good decision to marry him. We just both responded dramatically to the stress involved in the decision and wanted to do the right thing so badly that we worked ourselves into knots.

The coincidence of my contacting her on the day her husband had proposed and the bond we shared with our out-of-character reactions helped me to calm down and take stock. It was the reassurance I needed to make the decision I wanted to make anyway—to proceed with my wedding.

If you have an unusual response to engagement anxiety, don't jump to conclusions. Please remember that you are not alone. It is a major, stressful life decision, and you aren't crazy. Everyone wants to make the right decision. Don't call it off just because you're sick with butterflies. Talk to a trusted friend, write in a journal, get a session or two with a well-respected therapist, talk to a mentor…do something before jumping to a negative conclusion and canceling your plans.

Be sensitive to how you relay your experiences to your new fiancé, because it could hurt his feelings if he knows that you're ill or hyperventilating. He wants you to be happy. During freak-out time you're happy, but you're also so confused and off balance that you don't know what to do. You've never felt this way before. If you try to tell him, he won't understand what you're talking about. Just lie low, and work it out slowly but surely.

WHEN SOMETHING REALLY *Is* WRONG

Some people have to end engagements because they know deep down that something isn't right and that they will regret their decision. Even if you seek professional help, it's ultimately your call, and nobody else can take responsibility for your choice.

During such a tense time, it can be hard to see straight, and people can more easily influence you to go in either direction, whether it's the correct path or not. You'll be more prone to panic, exaggeration, and emotionally colored thinking if you already have a wedding dress and ring. So it's really better to analyze problems earlier in the relationship, when there is less to lose and the pressure isn't so oppressive. But if you know you're making a mistake, bailing out is worth the inconvenience and potential embarrassment.

THE ROAD NOT TAKEN

Engagement can be a tense time because the approaching marital commitment is your biggest decision after, perhaps, years of dating. It carries a sense of finality with it. It can feel claustrophobic at times, even if you are happy. People who can't handle this tension may have commitment phobia.

Even those who aren't commitment-phobic can second-guess themselves. You might find your imagination wandering back to previous flames. Maybe you thought one of them was actually going to be your husband. What if you still have feelings for him? Perhaps you know you are making the right choice but need closure. Handle old passions with care. Don't make big decisions about your future based on a scar. The scar won't marry you or have kids with you.

Dealing with a desire for closure is dicey. Some women meet up with their ex-boyfriends before their engagement. This could be a good way to relearn what a jerk the guy was and move forward with the wedding with a feeling of certitude that they wouldn't have otherwise. But let's be real about this! If you aren't yet over a former flame, why in the world would you want to meet up with him and allow your hormones and emotions to potentially confuse you at such a critical moment in your life? Such a move could upset your fiancé and serve to tease your ex.

I heard about one girl who met up with an ex during her engagement for "closure" and got upset when he tried to make a move on her. Well, dang, woman, *you* asked to get together with him! He might have thought that she was really serious about coming back to him or, God forbid, starting some sort of affair. If I were a guy, I'd wonder about the true motivations behind one of these get-togethers. Think twice before instigating a meeting, and if you cannot keep yourself from pursuing it, make sure your fiancé knows about it and supports you in order to ward off any misinterpretations that might jeopardize the engagement.

CHURCH REGISTRATION

Do yourself a favor by formally registering with the church you want to get married in and building a friendship with a priest there before engagement. Your fiancé could also take the responsibility. This way you won't be treated like a stranger and quizzed about your intentions, your faith, and your relationship quite so suspiciously when it's time to get married. Or if a parish guideline needs to be bent to accommodate your wishes, it can happen.

People from all walks of life choose churches simply because they seek beautiful architecture for their wedding. This is why church staff might be wary if you call about marriage prep and potential wedding dates and they don't know you. They might even have a rule about how long you must be a parishioner before they will support your wedding. Churches try to limit the number of weddings they host, and the limitations can be enormously unhelpful for brides-to-be.

In some churches, choices will already be made for you, which can be difficult for some brides to accept. When I lived in Washington, D.C., where there are breathtaking Catholic churches every few blocks, I had at least five within walking distance. Being unmarried, I had attended all of them at different times for special events and built meaningful friendships with clergy all over town. Nevertheless, when it came time to plan my wedding, the churches tended to adhere strictly to registration and parish boundaries.

Initially I approached a parish that is right next to where I was born. I thought, "This is the closest to a true home parish that I can get." It was also a good location for out-of-town wedding guests, because a hotel was next door. My former spiritual director had met with me there as well. Unfortunately, my spiritual director had been transferred months before I began my inquiries, and the new pastor would not budge an inch on parish boundary rules. I thought churches would be more eager to preside over weddings, but I discovered that if you live over the parish line, they might not be interested or able to help you.

I tried again at a magnificent church where I had once helped out with classes. It also had a hotel steps away. This pastor budged a bit more, but it still wasn't enough. His church was booked for a year or two, and only one day was available to us.

This priest told us that even if a family had used the church for weddings for generations, it wouldn't matter. Registration and parish boundaries are primary, and emotional attachments and relationships are secondary. It might all come down to registration and parish boundaries. So if you have your heart set on a particular Catholic parish, move into the community before you're engaged. This will help immensely.

Finally, we approached my home parish, which didn't have many weddings on the books. My parish was not on the best block, and the hotels were not as close, so it was not as desirable in some ways. But I found silver linings, and God was there for us. My former spiritual director concelebrated the Nuptial Mass with the pastor. It was also a little Italian parish—and I was marrying an Italian-American. They had a talented Italian musician. Additionally, there was a St. Padre Pio prayer group there the day of my wedding, so I felt as if my beloved Padre Pio was there, watching over us.

While things will usually work out for a couple trying to get married in the Church, some people experience profound difficulties if they have the misfortune of living in a parish that is booked for over a year and is inflexible with their schedule. I have heard of couples feeling blocked from receiving the sacraments, which is upsetting. If this happens, consider checking with your parents' church, as it is usually acceptable for a bride to come back home to her family's parish and hold the wedding there. For example, we knew a bride who lived in New York City but got married in New Jersey, where her parents owned a home. A location change like this may not be convenient or preferred by everyone, but it could be a way to get to the altar in a reasonable time frame.

chapter fourteen

HERE COMES THE BRIDE

Planning a wedding is a huge undertaking. I did everything I could to minimize stress. Since I knew what I wanted, I made most decisions independently, free from a committee. I also didn't want a huge wedding party. One matron of honor and her children serving as the flower girl and ring bearer were enough for me. If I had to do it again, I would do it the same way.

Many brides, however, opt to have lots of helpers or happen to have a large family. If you want lots of helpers, that typically means lots of bridesmaids, which translates into a bigger wedding. Keep that in mind. A bigger event means that someone is going to have to lead the team too, so if that won't be you, carefully choose someone who is responsible, trustworthy, and organized.

If you feel compelled to choose a sister as matron or maid of honor but worry that she may not be up to the tasks for whatever reason, entrust someone else with the real planning responsibilities and make her a bridesmaid. Most of the negative stories I hear about stuff spiraling out of control stem from a chaotic team of helpers, so choosing wisely will help you be a serene bride.

Hiring a wedding planner is becoming a popular option. Some wedding planners advertise that the discounts they can get on such things as flowers and catering make up for the fees they charge. This may or may not be true. If you know you don't have time to manage a huge event though, it might be the way to go. The best weddings are a true reflection of the bride and her groom, so don't get so detached from your wedding ceremony that you fail to personalize it, make it special, or remain close to the true meaning and spirituality behind it.

THE DRESS

My parents didn't get married in a church, and my mom didn't wear a wedding dress. I had no photos of any of my female relatives in wedding gowns. Neither of my grandmothers told me about their weddings. I hadn't attended a family wedding. So as far as I was concerned, I was the first family member in recent memory to have shopped for a wedding dress. During one of my trips to the bridal shop, my mom dropped me off and drove away. That's how alone I was!

Before you shop for your dress, read articles about body types and pick something that works for you, rather than the latest fad. Many dresses these days are sleeveless or strapless; if that strikes you as immodest, check online stores and remember that you can have some designs altered and fitted for sleeves and straps. Although you will feel the pressure to buy something, you won't need to settle for a dress that you don't like if you allow ample time for your search.

I chose a dress that harked back to my Mediterranean ancestry. (I'm half Greek.) It was a flowing gown that mirrored the style of ancient Greek and Roman statues. I had straps added.

Even though I was doing it without much help and zero experience, the appearance of the same dress on magazine covers after I had bought it confirmed that the fashion world approved of my choice. Phew!

I don't recommend buying a dress before you are even engaged, assuming, "Oh, that's the most beautiful dress I'll ever see. By the time I get engaged, it will be gone." I had this thought once when I was gazing at a dress through a store window. It was before I even met my husband. I don't remember the dress exactly, but I know that the one I bought for my wedding looked nothing like it. Styles change, and your own eye for fashion changes, so be patient and shop when it's time.

Is It Really Your Day?

When you get engaged, people will say of the wedding, "It's your day!" It will be spoken softly with the utmost sincerity by some and shouted with shrill excitement by others. I was very fortunate in some ways, because my parents didn't put any fishhooks in me. What I mean is that they didn't require anything of me when I got married or hold me hostage to their expectations. I could have done anything with my wedding, and they would have been supportive. Most women seem to have someone close to them who has an expectation or requirement, however.

One of my top lessons learned is that your wedding day doesn't belong only to you. Accept this early on, and you won't be a "Bridezilla." Getting married in a church environment, with family and friends in attendance, is just as much for the congregation, the body of Christ, as it is for you. People want to share your joy and be part of your life. I had my photographer take portraits of many of my guests at the reception, because I had learned by that time that the wedding also was about them.

Deciding which demands to meet can be a sensitive subject, especially if you and the groom are footing the bill. These days more couples are paying for a large portion of the wedding, but families and friends haven't necessarily adjusted their expectations accordingly. In our case I had to make a traditional wedding happen to please everyone but do it on a budget and keep us out of debt. Saying no to family demands isn't always a bad thing, but you should try to be accommodating, especially when guests travel great distances to be with you on your wedding day.

To an extent, the "it's your day" chatter is unfair. The groom can get cut out of the planning against his will. It's his day too. My husband, much to my surprise, wanted to be included in the planning. Your guy might want the same.

Learning Who the Kindred Spirits Are

An engagement will change your life in many ways. Aside from leading to marriage, it may change your relationships with others. Watch who RSVPs and who doesn't. Even people you have traveled long distances to see or you thought you had a bond with might not make the effort for your special day—for no particular reason. When some of my surprises were setting in, I mentioned it at work. My boss said, "We had that happen too! Yes, it can be surprising." You might be hurt, but use it as an opportunity to learn who the kindred spirits in your life really are.

Contracting With Friends and Family for Services

A friend of mine offered to provide some photography services to me for the wedding. There was no formal contract. A misunderstanding occurred about the terms, and the friendship ended as a result. This problem was probably avoidable.

Get any agreements with your friends and family in writing before the big day. Don't be fussing over terms verbally during the big event. With photography make sure you understand the copyright agreement that you are signing. Weddings are big business and yet tightly budgeted affairs, so if there is any question about an exchange of money, tempers can flare.

One communications professional told me that she even writes down agreements with her parents when money is involved. She tactfully explains it to them by saying, "This relationship is so important to me that I want to do this properly and avoid any misunderstandings." That's a diplomatic way of handling it! She watched someone conduct business on gentlemen's agreements alone, and it led to legal problems, so she changed her personal practices. Miscommunication is blind to friendships and family ties. Make sure everyone is firmly planted on the same page before the wedding.

The Ceremony

A Catholic wedding must take place in a church unless the bishop has granted a dispensation. It can either be very simple and low-key or quite opulent. Both you and your fiancé should be comfortable with the level of formality of the ceremony. While a well-rehearsed event may be someone's dream come true, it can make the other nervous and more likely to fold under the pressure. You want to find a compromise and not put either person in a situation that feels too out of place.

Familiarity with your venue can ease anxieties. I think this is one reason, aside from parish boundaries, that some women choose to get married at their childhood churches. Aside from the fact that the bride's family might foot the bill for the wedding, feeling at home is comforting when you are stressed out.

Many parishes will invite you to attend weddings at their church before your own wedding date to help you better visualize how it will all look on your big day. It's a good idea to take them up on this offer or to attend Mass there a few times if this isn't your home church. This might seem obvious, but it's worth mentioning, since some people choose a historic location or church with a long family history that they don't regularly attend.

Summer is wedding season. Go to weddings, even if you are still unhappily single, because they will give you ideas for your own wedding someday. The homilies will remind you what real marriage is about.

Since we chose to get married in a Catholic Nuptial Mass, the exchange of vows and rings happened in the middle of Mass. We could have chosen to get married without the Mass, however. There are meaningful ways to personalize a ceremony that don't include butchering the vows or doing anything irreverent. We had candles made with names of deceased relatives so they could be placed on the altar and remembered in prayer. Any time you receive a sacrament, Jesus and the angels are paying special attention, so I wanted to take full advantage of the occasion!

A professional organist who was also a vocalist helped me create the perfect music lineup. It's important to see how the music affects you emotionally before the big day. For instance, I couldn't handle "Here Comes the Bride." It was too intense and Hollywood-ish. However, I loved the dignified "The Prince of Denmark March," which Princess of Wales Diana used in her wedding. My maiden name is Welch, and the name reflects some Welsh ancestry, so this choice meant a lot to me. I walked down with a crown on my head and an ornate veil, and I felt very British at that moment. I also incorporated the "Prayer to St. Francis," sung in Italian, for my husband, whose patron saint is St. Francis.

Don't overcomplicate your ceremony. A guy told me about a relative who wanted a different song for every person in her wedding party who walked down the aisle. It was a disaster because the music couldn't be switched fast enough. Keep it simple and elegant, and rely on the advice of the experienced professionals you work with.

One more thing: Walking down the aisle is anxiety-provoking. Unless you plan to eliminate this tradition, dealing with the aisle is an almost universal experience in Western culture. One thing I did to relieve my jitters was to have my girlfriends gather around me and pray before entering the church. This was very soothing, and I highly recommend it!

Putting on a Good Show: The Reception

There is enormous pressure to script weddings, especially receptions, according to modern traditions. I successfully negotiated myself out of entertainment-oriented traditions I didn't like. For example, I dislike the garter toss that most couples do at their reception. It's embarrassing to me, and I couldn't overcome my modesty to do it. So I explained my predicament to my husband during our engagement and was able to forgo it.

I also picked up an aversion to dancing. I don't know why or how, since I adore music of many kinds, but that's just the way it is. Unfortunately, my husband really wanted to dance. I managed to work out a deal where I danced with him before the wedding, and the photographer got photos of that. From speaking to others I know I'm not the only one who questions the value of hiring a DJ, especially if the bride or groom doesn't even want to dance. We had Frank Sinatra music playing in the background instead, and that was good enough for us.

You might want to incorporate some traditions into your reception if it's a big event, but it's also important that they not leave you red-faced. You and your fiancé can reach a compromise and keep guests entertained.

We ended up doing OK. I had the most gorgeous flowers I have ever seen, a lovely dress, a fabulous cake, and hair and makeup done by a makeup artist who worked with first ladies and celebrities. We had a nice reception with great food on a boat that cruised between northern Virginia and Washington, D.C. I have watched friends borrow ideas from our wedding. Looking back, I'm glad we did it the way we did. We never say, "If only...". That's how you want to feel.

THE DEVIL'S LAST STAND
The day or so immediately before the ceremony is the devil's last chance to keep you single. Since I try to surround myself with positive people and conversation, I didn't want to believe that evil forces would try to interfere with my wedding. Regardless, a series of bizarre mishaps right before the event made me wonder. The experience made me ponder the spiritual forces that can keep girls single.

The night of our rehearsal, I was calmly going about my business in my little apartment, enjoying my last few hours of peace and solitude. I started a relaxing bath and thought about the new dress I was going to wear to the rehearsal. The phone rang, and I ignored it. Then my Zen-like calm was shattered by a frantic voice mail from my fiancé, which I heard in the bath. He was in the parking lot of the Baltimore Washington International Airport and couldn't find his keys. He thought they had been stolen.

I was irritated! I called back and said, "Why are you doing this last-minute? How could you lose your keys? I'm sorry, I can't help you; you're going to have to get a cab and deal with this yourself." He didn't want a cab, and the phone call ended in a screaming match over how I thought he should suck up the cab fare because there was no way he would make it to the rehearsal otherwise.

His best man drove a long distance to get him. As they started driving toward D.C. together, the sky opened, and it rained harder than it had all year. Traffic slowed to a crawl because visibility was very poor. Some people pulled over to the side of the road. It took Attilio and his best man forever to get to the church, and they were hours late.

The rehearsal dinner went OK, although Attilio's father wasn't able to make it. It's traditional for the groom's parents to host the dinner, so this was a disappointment. Then my fiancé's credit card didn't work because of an error by the card company.

After the dinner he had to have the lock to his apartment changed since his key was missing. There was an issue with getting his tux too. It was the worst day ever, and we wondered how on earth a day could be that horrible. You hear that something always goes wrong, but this was bad.

The day of the wedding, I once again tried to have a relaxing time. I decided to go to Starbucks for breakfast. For the first time ever, the handle to the front door of my apartment building broke. One needed a screwdriver to pry the door open or someone to kindly let you in. Luckily I didn't get locked out, but I had to call for repairs. I said, "Don't use me as the point of contact for this, because I'm getting married today, but that's why it needs to be fixed ASAP. I'm not getting locked out when I go to the salon this afternoon!"

I wasn't the only one experiencing difficulties. My matron of honor came over and told me that she'd found that she had two left or right shoes, so she'd had to scramble that morning to get a correct pair of shoes. Imagine if she hadn't checked before she left her house, or if the store didn't have her size.

Traffic was bad, and we started the wedding a little late because people were stuck on the roads. The wedding itself was beautiful, but as it ended, a huge thunderclap struck outside, and it started pouring rain. It was as if Satan was saying, "Bah, humbug, they got married anyway." Or maybe Jesus was saying, "See, Satan—they persevered!" Whatever it meant, people remembered it.

Matrimony is uniquely blessed by God. To my way of thinking, so is the often-lengthy dating process that leads up to it—in spite of, or perhaps because of, the negative experiences along the way. It's worth a few trials to be able to say, "I do," before God and his Church!

epilogue

MAINTAINING BALANCE

A week before a friend was due to tie the knot with his bride, my husband asked him if he was nervous or had any misgivings. He said, "I'm worried that I won't have any alone time." While some people mock the whole concept of "me time," it has its place.

Couples may worry about maintaining a healthy balance of togetherness and independence and wonder how to achieve a good spiritual blend as well. It's easy to overcomplicate the topic of balance, when simplicity is often the best answer.

A Personal Relationship With God

Christians will often say, "A family that prays together stays together." Don't neglect your personal relationship with the Lord in favor of group prayer though. Make time for your own silent prayer and meditation, and if you have a crazy schedule, have conversations with God when you're running errands, or pray while walking or driving. Being personally anchored in God's love for you means that you'll always have a calm, safe place to retreat to when you're stressed out, when there is an argument, or when you need to recharge.

ALONE OR TOGETHER?

When we got married my husband and I put together an office space where our desks were identical and facing each other. We thought that marriage meant that we would always be together at home. The office didn't work so well! We had to move my desk to another room so I could concentrate. Sometimes, even when you get along famously with your significant other, you need independence.

Now we have separate office spaces. That can mean too much alone time, so we instant message each other or use an intercom system to talk if we're working on separate things. Other times we bring our laptops into the same room so we can pursue individual activities together.

While we have both a joint checking account and e-mail address, we also maintain our own accounts so we have a degree of personal freedom.

Experiment, be flexible, and be lighthearted about finding your balance. There are times for separateness and togetherness, and much will depend on your personalities.

. . . .

Attilio: If you are younger when you get married, it may seem odd having separate "things," but when you have lived alone beyond college life and established an independent personality, that part of you shouldn't be thrown away when you join in marriage. You'll most likely feel repressed if you attempt to.

Having a level of independence and a corner to go off to for my individual rest is something I cherish, and I know my wife does too. Everyone is different, so don't read into it too much if a man asks for some of his own space. Having a "man cave" is healthy, as long as your man spends time with you, too, and isn't always alone.

. . . .

DETACHMENT

A photographer friend, Marc, inquired about my husband's progress in getting his own photography gigs. I said that he had advertised recently, but that I didn't know how quickly things would progress. I explained that when I have a goal, I turbo-charge it full force. My husband is more laid back and does things in his own time.

Marc said, "That detachment is very good for a marriage. You didn't complain about his being 'slow' or anything like that; you just let him follow his own pace."

Husbands and wives need space to do things their own way. This can keep things on an even keel. While some hobbies can be pursued together, others are better left separate if you have different ways of doing things or having fun.

This kind of respect also helps when you need to ask "permission" to make a purchase or do something. Allowing the other person some independence makes those talks easier.

SOCIAL INVOLVEMENT

Once you've paired up, your spouse can be your main company. You always have someone to talk to and a best friend nearby.

At the same time your spouse can't fill every social need for you. Making some time for friends and group activities is healthy and helps prevent the problem of making excessive demands on your significant other.

Ups and Downs

It concerns me when singles ask couples, "Are you happy?" If they don't get an immediate "Yes!" they're disappointed. The question reveals an unrealistic expectation.

The most important thing to remember about relationships is that they have ups and downs. There is a natural ebb and flow. One year could be tough, and another year could be easy. A downer Monday doesn't mean date night on Friday won't make up for it. One argument doesn't necessarily equal a breakup. If you pressure yourselves to be high on each other's presence 24-7, you could negatively assess what is in fact a fine relationship.

Try to remember the big picture and see your relationship from a bird's-eye view. Relationships are journeys, not destinations, and marriage is special because you grow together with your spouse over a lifetime.

Invoking Protection

Catholics honor St. Michael as a protecting angel. This traditional prayer invokes his defense in any situation, including dating and marriage:

Saint Michael the Archangel,
defend us in battle.
Be our protection against the wickedness and snares of
the devil.
May God rebuke him, we humbly pray;
and do thou, O Prince of the Heavenly Host—
by the divine power of God—
cast into hell Satan and all the evil spirits,
who roam throughout the world seeking the ruin of
souls.
Amen.

1. Richard Fry and D'Vera Cohn, "New Economics of Marriage: The Rise of Wives" (Executive Summary), *Pew Research Center*, January 19, 2010, http://pewsocialtrends.org.

2. Amy Bonaccorso, "Catholic Singles Feel Angst," the *Washington Times*, November 20, 2008, www.washingtontimes.com. The man I interviewed was named Chris Corrish.

3. Bureau of Labor Statistics, "Women in the Labor Force: A Databook" (2009 Edition), table 11, p. 28, www.bls.gov.

4. Fry and Cohn.

5. Laura Moncur's Motivational Quotations, Quotation 39152, http://thinkexist.com.

6. Tom Hoopes, "Breaking Vows: When Faithful Catholics Divorce," *Crisis* magazine, July/August 2004, http://insidecatholic.com.

7. Jennifer Baker, "Divorce Rate," www.divorcerate.org.

8. Michael J. Glantz, et al., "Gender disparity in the rate of partner abandonment in patients with serious medical illness," *Cancer*, vol. 115, no. 22 (November 15, 2009), pp. 5237–5242, www3.interscience.wiley.com.

9. Bureau of Labor Statistics, "Economic News Release, American Time Use Survey Summary, 2008 Results," table 1, www.bls.gov.

10. Bonaccorso, interview with Kim McKenzie.

11. Henry Cloud and John Townsend, *Safe People: How to Find Relationships That Are Good for You and Avoid Those That Aren't* (Grand Rapids: Zondervan, 1995), p. 34.

12. MythBusters Results, April 11, 2007, Voice Flame Extinguisher episode, http://mythbustersresults.com.

13. Hill Harper, *CNN* interview by T.J. Holmes, September 6, 2009, http://newsroom.blogs.cnn.com.

14. Vanessa Camden, "Cohabitation: Are You Ready?" *The Examiner*, October 23, 2009, www.examiner.com. The original data were derived from a report of a study by Galena K. Rhoades, Scott M. Stanley, and Howard J. Markman, "The Pre-Engagement Cohabitation Effect: A Replication and Extension of Previous Findings," *Journal of Family Psychology*, vol. 23, no. 1 (February 2009), pp. 107–111.

ABOUT THE AUTHOR

AMY BONACCORSO converted to Catholicism in college
and overcame many dating disappointments before she found
her husband, Attilio. Now, she shares her lessons learned with
singles so they can take charge of their lives and expertly navigate the dating scene. Amy resides in the Washington, D.C.,
area and is an accomplished communications specialist with the
U.S. government.